ADVANCE PRAISE FOR

It's Not *All About You!*

Daniel Cohen's first book is a tour de force that was born out of his personal and professional experience as well as his groundbreaking research in the area of humility. *It's* Not *All About You!* is not your typical "feel good" book with little practical effects on your daily life. This book is in essence a roadmap for deep joy and fulfilling personal development. Cohen's idea to organize it into multiple paths is brilliant. Those paths not only lead to wisdom but also offer a sort of personal life curriculum that people can embrace to become better selves. The crescendo of data, information and knowledge about the practical aspects of humility included in the paths makes this book a must read for people who are intentional about becoming more productive, more altruistic, and more effective in dealing with life challenges. *It's* Not *All About You!* is ideal for people who are looking for a serious and practical personal development book. It can also be very helpful for psychotherapists who work with patients dealing with issues related to humility. Ministers may use it to teach about humility, and college professors can use it on their social work or psychology classes. Even business leaders should encourage their employees to read this exceptional book.

—PASTOR JEAN-FRITZ GUERRIER

I loved this book! Not only did it teach me how to cope with life's ups and downs better, it made me laugh many times. The author's humorous anecdotes combined with his sense of humor were a big plus. That said, the most important thing for me was the 70 humility paths or what the author calls "mental happiness tools." They made me look at life in a different way. Now I'm not so mad at the things other people do, and I find my anxiety has decreased as I now accept my proper place in the universe as someone who is both special and yet just a part of the great mosaic of life. I couldn't recommend this book more highly! Thank you! Thank you!

—ANA CARRASQUILLO, accountant

In these times of rampant egocentricism and unbridled consumerism, little is devoted to that virtue known as humility. Thankfully, Daniel Cohen's new book entitled *It's* Not *All About You! The Secret Joy of Practical Humillity* brings humility to the forefront and points out how being humble can improve our lives. Daniel Cohen who is a Protestant minister and social worker, draws from his personal experiences, his knowledge of religion and his training as a therapist to provide examples, insights and paths to cultivate humility in our everyday lives at home and at work. This deceptively simple book filled with humor contains paths and exercises for developing humility which leads to better inter-personal relationships and happier lives. This is a book meant to be shared and reread.

—MARIANO ALEMANY, architect

This book is a true *tour de force* in humility. I found every one of the paths right on. Because I am such a critical person, I was surprised that I didn't object to one. So from a content point of view—well done. Also, I liked your style and your humor.

—BOB JAPENGA, author of *An Introductory Guide to Listening Prayer* and founder of Listening to God Ministries

It's *Not* All About You!

The Secret Joy
of Practical Humility

THE HAPPINESS THROUGH HUMILITY SERIES

DANIEL AARON COHEN,
MSJ, MDIV, LCSW

Contents

Preface.. vii

Introduction.. 1

Section I: Humility and Modern Society 9

Section II: Paths That Help Us Not Think Too Highly
Of Ourselves 25

Section III: Paths That Help Us Not Think Too Low
Of Ourselves 131

Section IV: Paths That Help Us Not Think Of Ourselves
Too Often 141

Section V: The Eight Paths of Blessing God.................... 177

Appendix A: The Humility Paths (Or "Mental Happiness Tools")
And The Exercises That Go With Them............................ 195

Appendix B: Recommended Spiritual Reading 212

Appendix C: Two Poems for Spiritual Growth.............. 213

Appendix D: Some Excellent Quotations About Humility 216

About the Author 219

PREFACE

"For me there is only the traveling on paths that have heart,
on any path that may have heart. There I travel, and the only
worthwhile challenge is to traverse its full length.
And there I travel looking, looking, breathlessly."

— CARLOS CASTANEDA,
THE TEACHINGS OF DON JUAN: A YAQUI WAY OF KNOWLEDGE

These words, spoken by Don Juan, the Native American Wiseman Carlos Castaneda writes about in *The Teachings of Don Juan: A Yaqui Way of Knowledge* sum up my reason for writing *It's Not All About You! The Secret Joy of Practical Humility.*

Living from a place of humility and writing about humility is, for me, a path with heart.

You see, I believe humility is not only the key to happiness but the key to being a better human being. For while some seek money, they do so in the pursuit of happiness—so their wealth is only valuable in its ability to make them happy.

Humility makes you happy as it takes away self-consciousness and helps you accept Life's difficulties while making you more grateful for Life's blessings. But humility goes beyond happiness as it makes you a blessing to others and—for those who believe in One—a blessing to your Maker as well.

This book was a long time coming. It started about 15 years ago when the pastor at the church I attended suggested I write a book. And while this book is for believers and non-believers alike, it was this nudge that got me thinking about writing a book on humility—a subject I approach as a psychotherapist and a Christian pastor. Although I self-identify as a Jewish-Christian with Buddhist tendencies, I've gone out of my way to make this book palatable to my atheist and agnostic readers as well. I was once one of you, after all, and so I have saved most of my "God talk" for the very end.

Why on Earth did it take me so long to write this book? The short answer is that I had to start from scratch. For while many of the ideas are universal, I know of no book about humility like it. So, while it draws inspiration from the twelve steps of Alcoholics Anonymous' *Twelve Steps and Twelve Traditions*, the Dalai Lama's *Essential Teachings* and Michael Singer's *The Untethered Soul,* this book, with its essay on Consumerism and the humility paths that follow, is quite unique—and represents the culmination of a great deal of thinking, researching, organizing, writing and re-writing.

Fortunately, the work that went into *It's* Not *all About You!* has also laid the foundation for the next two books which complete the three-volume set. These books are on humility paths that help readers to 1) *Accept* those things we don't like about life that we cannot change, and 2) be *Grateful* for everything we do like about life. Acceptance and Gratitude are the basis of the second and third part of my definition of humility.

Now a word to those of you who are reading this book because someone has given it to you as a not-so-subtle hint that you need to become more humble. You should know that the person who gave you this book probably needs it as much—if not more—than you do. After all, it is the humble soul that will read this book and grow, while the less humble soul will feel confident that whatever problems they are experiencing in their relationship with you are your problems, not theirs.

Moving on, let me give you an idea of how the book is structured. The book starts with an introduction which lays out why humility is so essential to our happiness. This is followed by four main sections. The first section is an essay that lays out why we as a global society are further from humility than ever before. This includes a discussion of the two questions society has us asking ourselves to get us to buy more stuff to make us happy.

This essay is followed by the meat of the book which is comprised of 70 different humility paths—or mental tools—that will help you put yourself in perspective. These paths will help you 1) not think too highly or yourself. 2) not think too low of yourself and 3) not think too often of yourself. Taking yourself out of the center of the Universe and putting your ego in its proper place frees you from the selfishness and self-consciousness that lead to the anxiety, depression and anger we moderns suffer from. Internalizing these paths will make you humbler, happier and more successful, as others will see the change in you and want to help you succeed. This will be true in both your personal and professional relationships. Over the course of the book, you will discover that humility has nothing to do with weakness and everything to do with appreciating and enjoying your life without stress.

You will also notice that I employ my offbeat sense of humor throughout the book, mostly be stealing other people's jokes (it has been said that good comedians write their own material, while great ones steal theirs). This is why I open up the book with a humorous humility quiz that has been particularly well-received at my speaking engagements.

The Humility Quiz

1. When someone criticizes you in an unkind way, do you:

   a) Remind yourself as the Dalai Lama suggests to be thankful for your enemies as they reveal truths about you that help you grow.

   b) Remind yourself of what Jesus said about turning the other cheek.

   c) Apply Elvis Costello's line "I used to be disgusted but now I try to be amused."

   d) Curse them out.

   e) Go shopping for handguns.

2. When you are stuck in a traffic jam, do you:

   a) Look at this as an opportunity for prayer and meditation.

   b) Think about Michael Singer's line "Everything will be okay as soon as you are okay with everything."

   c) Curse God out for putting you in this traffic jam.

   d) Reach for some benzos.

3. When you are given bad service in a restaurant do you:

   a) Remind yourself that it's not all about you.

   b) Look at this as an opportunity to practice forgiveness.

   c) Curse out the waiter.

   d) Talk to the manager and try to get the waiter fired.

4. When your boss gets on your last nerve do you:

    a) Remind yourself that he or she is only human too.

    b) Look at the positive things your boss does.

    c) Go to HR and try to get them canned.

    d) Call your local hit man.

5. When your husband or wife does something unfair, do you:

    a) Remind yourself to be thankful to have a mate who puts up with your mess.

    b) Remind yourself to be grateful you have a mate when many others don't.

    c) Remember your mate's good qualities.

    d) Lash out in anger.

    e) Have an affair.

6. When you wake up in the morning and get ready for work, are you:

    a) Grateful that you have a job when there are others who don't.

    b) Eager to share your love with the clients and co-workers you have the opportunity to work with.

    c) Upset that you have to go to work instead of having your own reality show like the Kardashians.

    d) Counting the days until retirement.

7. When there's someone in your life you don't like, the best thing to do about it is:

   a) Pray for them.

   b) Look for opportunities to show them kindness.

   c) Look for opportunities to make them look bad.

   d) Say bad things about them behind their back.

8. When someone gets promoted ahead of you, your response is:

   a) To be glad for them, knowing that what God can do for them, He can do for you.

   b) File a grievance.

   c) Throw darts at their picture.

9. When you compare yourself to others do you:

   a) Thank God that you have more than some who have less than you.

   b) Wish you had as much as people who have a little more than you have.

   c) Wish you had your own reality show.

   d) Get angry and kick the dog.

So how did you do? Don't worry if you didn't do so well. Neither did I. It will be our little secret.

INTRODUCTION

I didn't write this book because I'm so humble, but because I need humility as much as anyone. In fact, I sometimes think that if my ego applied for statehood it would become the fourth largest state in the union—right after Alaska, California and Texas!* However, there are other times—times which are growing more frequent—when I feel in touch with a humility that is slowly transforming me from the neurotic, selfish and self-centered egotist I can be when I'm "in self" into someone much better. For when I'm feeling humble, I am at peace with the world. I'm relaxed, confident and loving. I'm thinking about how I can be a blessing to others instead of focusing on myself. Humility grounds me. It helps me appreciate life more. It keeps me from worrying about what others think of me.

But what, precisely, *is* humility? I'd like to propose the following three-fold definition:

1. *Humility is not thinking too highly of ourselves, too low of ourselves, or thinking about ourselves too often.* (What we'll call Traditional Humility)

2. *Humility is* **accepting** *everything you don't like about life that you cannot change.* And

3. Humility is *being* **grateful** *for everything you DO like about life.*

It's Not *all About You!* focuses on paths that lead to "traditional humility." Separate books on Acceptance and Gratitude are in the works.

---

* Humility insists I confess I lifted this line from an old *Saturday Night Live* episode lampooning sports journalist Bryant Gumbel.

Now Let's Look At What Humility Is Not

Humility is not weakness. Being humble does not mean letting people walk all over you. Dr. Martin Luther King was a humble man of God, yet he stood up for African Americans. Pope Francis is humble, but he fights for human rights. Jesus was humble, but He took a whip and kicked the money changers out of the temple for making "[His] father's house a den of thieves."

No, humility is not letting others mistreat you. For doing so not only hurts you, it hurts them as well. It is entirely appropriate to respect your own boundaries while helping others learn the important lesson that they should respect other people's boundaries too—as long as this is done out of love.

☙

Now that we know what humility is and what it is not, let's briefly discuss some of the advantages of attaining more of it.

Let's start with a simple equation:

First off, humility is better than happiness and happiness is better than money. Let me explain. People want money because they think it will make them happy—which it may or may not. Therefore happiness is more important than money. Humility will definitely make you happier, as we will see, but it will also make you a better person, which will make others happier and God happier.

While humility (or the lack of it) has been central to my life, you may not suffer from the same problems I do. You may never be anxious or depressed, self-centered or egotistical, self-conscious or selfish. If you're wondering how humility can help *you*, ask yourself which of the following statements are true for you:

- I want to enjoy life more than I already do.
- I want to be healthier—both mentally and physically. I want to live longer.

- I want to have deeper, more meaningful relations with my family and friends.
- I want to be less concerned about what others think of me.
- I want to be less selfish.
- I want to be more secure and confident. I want to have a better marriage.
- I want to have a better love life.
- I want to have better relationships with the people I work with.
- I want to get along with my mother-in-law without hiring a hit man.
- I want to please my Higher Power.
- I want to be a better person.

If you said "yes" to any of these statements, this book is for you. If you're thinking that everyone would want these things, that's because *It's* Not *all About You!* was written with a very specific audience in mind: People who want to live happier, more fulfilling lives.

At this point you're probably thinking: "Now seriously Dan, how can humility do all of these things for me?"

First Off, Humility Is Practical

Unlike products which promise to change your life on the outside (you know, the ones that say you'll lose 100 pounds in 30 days or make a small fortune in real estate while lounging around in your sweatpants), humility changes your life from the *inside*. It challenges you to *appreciate what you have more* rather than seeking more to appreciate. To focus on giving rather than taking. To focus on others rather than self. Humility does not promise to change the things that are in your external world, but changing your inner world will inevitably lead to such changes as well.

If, for example, humility helps you do the dishes and clean the bathroom, your wife will want to be more romantic (this is a well-researched fact). If your humility helps you be sweeter to your husband he will be more likely to do the dishes and clean the bathroom.

Likewise, if your humility helps you work under your boss without complaining, if it helps you get along better with your co-workers and treat your subordinates with greater respect, it may well lead to the promotion you're looking for. People *like* humble people and want to help them succeed. So it shouldn't surprise you that the most successful CEOs tend to share a common trait: Humility.

Humility changes us within. Beyond sex and money, humility will help you live a longer, healthier, happier life. Stress is the number one source of disease, and the more humility you have, the more you're able to accept life as it is. Humility will help you relate better to friends and family and can even help you raise your teenager with more serenity. In fact, it is so closely tied to serenity that you can easily substitute the word "humility" for "serenity" in the serenity prayer. "Lord, give me the *humility* to accept the things I cannot change, the courage to change the things I can, and the wisdom to know the difference."

Imagine never having to worry about anything ever again. If you had enough humility that would, by definition, be your reality. For humility means accepting life as it unfolds, being content with what you already have. And while total humility may be out of reach, the more humility you develop, the less anxious you become. Anxiety comes from worrying about the future. If you're open to accepting whatever life has in store for you, you have no worries.

Humility is also key to your relationship with your Higher Power. In his classic, *Humility: The Journey Towards Holiness*, Andrew Murray writes: "Humility is not so much a virtue along with the others, but is the root of all, because it alone takes the right attitude before God and allows Him, as God, to do all."

This raises the question:

"If humility is so beneficial, why haven't I heard more about it before?"

If you haven't seen all the advertisements for humility on TV and in magazines or heard our politicians touting humility's merits, it's because we live in a society that doesn't appear to value humility much. So while we may value humility in our personal relationships, our society as a whole suggests happiness is found in getting new things to appreciate rather than learning to better appreciate what you already have. While it may be more pronounced in the West, this is a global phenomenon, with people all over the world clamoring for newer gadgets—and newer spouses—instead of being happy with the ones they have. Humility is not popular in Western society because it runs counter to its basic assumptions of what makes you happy.

Society says: He who dies with the most toys wins.

Humility says: Be happy with the toys you have.

Society says: Compare yourselves to those who have more and catch up to them so you can be happy too.

Humility says: Be grateful that you have more than some.

We live in a self-centered society. Everything is about me, me, me. We scream "Look at me!" on Facebook and "Listen to me!" on Twitter. We even have a popular magazine called *Self!* This causes all kinds of problems because we are finite beings who will one day pass away. Thinking the world revolves around us is like believing the Sun revolves around the Earth, and focusing on Self makes us self-conscious, leading to anxiety and depression. As Michael Singer writes in his seminal work *The Untethered Soul*: "Your inner growth is completely dependent upon the realization that the only way to find peace and contentment is to stop thinking about yourself."

Another reason humility has a bad reputation is that it is misunderstood as weakness in a society which glorifies arrogance. I once had a boss who liked to say our team included a lot of "strong personalities" (that is mean and bossy people)—the strongest of which was her own. By phrasing it this way, my boss portrayed her character flaw as a strength. By her definition, Jesus, Gandhi and Dr. Martin Luther King didn't have strong personalities!

Next I'd like to focus on how humility is both timeless and timely Humility is a timeless virtue, as old as mankind. That humility is so undervalued today is precisely why we need it more than ever.

Yet there are signs humility's stock is on the rise. Not only do we have a humble Pope in Pope Francis, recently the most popular course at Harvard wasn't about business and economics, but "happiness." This is part of a young science called "Positive Psychology" which, like *It's Not all About You!* looks to optimize our happiness potential rather than simply cure mental illness.

What's more, the recent COVID-19 pandemic has humbled us both individually and as a species, reminding us that we are not the masters of our universe we thought we were.

Humility increases our happiness by helping us dial down our expectations of life. In his second book, *Perfect*, former Harvard professor Tal Ben-shahar says the most pervasive problem he came across when writing his first book, *Happier*, was an unrealistically high expectation of happiness.

Being happy comes not from turning life into one uninterrupted party, but 1) recognizing that life is not all about you, 2) accepting those distasteful things that we can't change, and 3) giving thanks for all the good in our lives—the three pillars of humility.

But if humility is related to happiness in that the humbler you are, the happier you become, it is much more than that. Humility goes beyond personal happiness as it benefits those around you. And the more you give to others the more you get back, giving you yet more to give, and so on.

Of course not everyone lacks humility. In addition to the humble people you know personally, there's one non-religious institution where humility is given its due. Can you guess where that is? If you said "Alcoholics Anonymous" you're right. The 12-step approach of AA is all about humility. In fact, AA founder Bill Wilson emphatically states, "The attainment of greater humility is the foundation principle of each of AA's twelve steps." AA is about fixing the underlying problems that lead alcoholics to drink and behave self-ishly. AA recognizes that beneath the addiction to alcohol lies an addiction to self. While this book isn't a 12-step program, to call it AA for the self-aholic would not be farfetched.

As the success of 12-step programs suggests, humility can be learned. Mark Twain said that when he was 14 he considered his father a fool, but by the time he was 21 he was amazed to see how much his father had grown. As anyone who has ever been a teenager knows, humility is something we learn over time. And while you can take decades to learn the humility life has to teach you, reading this book and practicing humility can make the path to a humbler, happier you quicker and easier than learning through the school of hard knocks alone.

SECTION I

Humility And Modern Society

"When science discovers the center of the universe,
a lot of people will be disappointed to find they are not it."

— BERNARD BAILY

As I mentioned in the introduction, my ego has been so large at times it could have successfully applied for statehood. So large that a deacon at Grace Gospel Church in Paterson, New Jersey—the church where I preached my first sermon—pulled me aside one day and said "Dan, it's not all about you." This phrase, spoken in love, would be one I would repeat much more emphatically—and with much less love—to my uncle in the same church years later.

Otherwise known for my meek temperament in church, my uncle Winston caused me to lose my cool one day.

You see, I'd gone to the church with a friend who was visiting from out of town. A friend who Winston had met the previous time she'd visited a year ago. As fate would have it, Winston, a man who was not known for holding his tongue, happened to be sitting in the pew right in front of us. So when Winston saw her, the first question he asked me was how long she had been here. When I told him "Three weeks," he took umbrage, feeling that, given his sense of self-importance, he should have been notified that my friend was in town—this despite the fact that they were merely casual acquaintances and nothing more. "THREE weeks!" Winston bellowed. "THREE weeks! She's been here THREE

WEEKS and no one has bothered to call me?!" I apologized as best I could, but Winston persisted for what seemed to be longer than the "three weeks" he was complaining about. Finally, thankfully, the service started and Winston halted his verbal smack down.

However, the *second* the service was over, Winston was back at it again.

"THREE WEEKS," he bellowed. "THREE —"

And before he could hit "weeks" again, I lit into him like a preacher into an unrepentant sinner:

"Winston," I yelled, "IT'S NOT ALL ABOUT YOU!"

"THREE WEEKS!"

"IT'S NOT ALL ABOUT YOU!" I yelled.

"Three weeks!"

"IT'S NOT ALL ABOUT YOU WINSTON!"

"Three –

"IT'S NOT ALL ABOUT YOU WINSTON!"

"weeks"

"IT'S NOT ALL ABOUT YOU WINSTON!"

At this point, people were staring. I didn't care. I was preaching my sermon. Winston kept muttering. I kept hitting my theme. Eventually I left him and went outside. I'll never forget the sight of Winston, twenty years my senior, hobbling down the stairs at the front of the church on his bad leg to tell me that if I ever embarrassed him like that again he'd punch me in my face.

Later we would make up, and we've never had a problem since. In fact, he is a great man of God and I respect him immensely. Still, I don't think Winston will ever forget the humiliation heaped on him that day. This reflects the law of humility and humiliation: that a little humility will keep you from a whole heap of humiliation.

The problem Winston and I share is not unique. Thinking "it's all about me" is modern mankind's bane. For while selfishness and self-consciousness are nothing new, both have reached epidemic proportions in today's society.

Why Now?
Consumerism: Our 21st Century Religion

Today the global religion that exerts the most influence over our lives is neither Christianity or Islam, Buddhism or Judaism, but "Consumerism." That is, the religion of materialism. This "religion" puts Self on the throne. In so doing, it creates gods out of those of us who, consciously or unconsciously, worship ourselves. Uncomfortably mortal gods who are constantly vying to improve our position in the pantheon by acquiring the fame and fortune Society says we must have. In this age of income inequality where we're Keeping up with the Kardashians as well as the Joneses, society has us asking ourselves two basic questions: "What can I get out of life—and am I getting enough?" and its kissing cousin "What do other people think of me?" These two questions lead to the self-centeredness that plagues modern Humankind, and are responsible for much of the misery in the world today.

The first question—"What can I get out of life—and am I getting enough?"—is the root cause of all selfishness, and leads to war, crime, gluttony, greed, hate and adultery. The second question—"What do other people think of me?"—is the root of our self-consciousness, and leads to anxiety, pride, envy and depression. These two questions are constantly running through our minds whether we realize it or not. Old as society, they have taken on new meaning in modern times where our "self"-obsession has reached epidemic proportions.

This raises the question...

Why Does Society Do This To Us?

Now to be clear I'm not suggesting some grand conspiracy hatched in a D.C. boardroom by a cadre of old white men smoking Cubans, swigging Jack Daniels and plotting our ultimate demise. No, I am suggesting something much simpler. Something that comes about as a matter of course. Consider: Two-thirds of our economy is driven by consumer spending. Consumerism's goal is to get us to buy new things. In order to do this, Society must convince us that we need more than we have. Advertisers "create a need" by a) making their products seem appealing ("What can I get out of life—and am I getting enough?") and b) making us feel inadequate with what we have ("What do other people think of me?"). Thus Society turns life into a competition where it's all about us.

The problem is that Society is focused not on our happiness, but on getting us to buy things that will "make us happy." We've been brainwashed to think that happiness comes from outward success. This is not true. In the documentary "Happy," Tim Kasser, Professor and Chair of Psychology at Knox College and author of *The High Price of Materialism* cites studies which show that while Americans are earning twice as much as they were 50 years ago, it hasn't made us any happier. Kasser reports that people who seek the intrinsic goals of personal growth, healthy relationships, and helping others tend to be happy, whereas people with the extrinsic goals of money, image and status are not.

That's because being selfish and self-conscious DON'T lead to happiness. This is counter-intuitive, as it would seem that looking out for our own self-interest would lead to the greatest satisfaction. But this is not how our Maker/evolution has created us. We were created to love one another, to work together and help each other. To cooperate as well as compete. The reason we are the most successful species on Earth is not because we are more competitive than other animals, but because we are able to cooperate at an unprecedented level, each of us sharing our own special gifts with one another.

We were designed so that the more happiness we create for others, the more happiness we get in return. In Buddhism and Hinduism, this is called "karma." In Christianity it is "you reap what you sow" and "do unto others as you would have them do unto you." In the common language of the streets it's "what goes around comes around." God/evolution has created us to be social animals, and has given us consciences. The Bible tells me that all of the 613 commandments found in the Old

Testament boil down to just two: Love God with all your heart and love your neighbor as yourself.

Unfortunately, our current civilization encourages us to focus on a more selfish path to happiness. Instead of encouraging us to love one another and develop a mind that can handle adversity without being disturbed, we try to maximize our pleasure and avoid pain by changing our circumstances or taking drugs or alcohol. The secret of personal growth is working on how we deal with challenges internally, whether through therapy, meditation, prayer or studying, and that takes a lot more effort than popping a pill or downing a shot of whiskey. But I'm preaching to the choir, as you're doing the work right now by reading this book.

Humility also isn't front and center in the 21st century because humility is bad for business-as-usual. While society tells you that you will be happier when you get more things, humility shows you how to be happier with the things you already have. Society tells you that new car, that new house, that new job, that new cell phone will make you happy. And while there's nothing wrong with nice things, the happiness you get from them is usually short-lived, in part because if you're not happy with what you have now, there's no guarantee you'll be happy when you get new things. Besides, getting new stuff only makes you happy temporarily. For once you have it, you soon become used to it and take it for granted. Then your mind goes on to focus on the next thing you "need" to be happy.

If you haven't figured it out already, there's always something newer and better out there that you haven't got yet. Besides, you may never get what you're striving for: Getting new things is something that is ultimately out of your control, as something could get in the way, including death—a subject that makes us mortal gods extremely uneasy.

Worry: Consumerism's High Pricetag

A recent study showed that emotional language had been on the decline throughout the 20th century with one notable exception: Use of the word "fear" has been growing since the 1980s—and that was *before* 9/11 and the COVID-19 virus took our anxiety into the stratus-fear (sorry, couldn't resist). Small wonder that, in any given year, 40 million Americans suffer from anxiety-related disorders while 284 million suffer worldwide, not to mention those who suffer from depressive disorders brought on by our fears.

If you are suffering from the anxiety and depression common to modern mankind, you are paying Consumerism's price tag. This anxiety and depression stem not only from our failure to become president, billionaire or superstar—nor is it just from having less than the guy one rung higher than you on the success ladder—but from the two basic fears that come from keeping up with the Kardashians and the Joneses: The fear of Embarrassment (which comes from worrying about what others think of us), and an intense fear of Death that comes from believing the world revolves around us, making our inevitable demise a tragedy of epic proportions. Fears which can be cured by a good dose of humility.

Comedian Jerry Seinfeld notes that the top two phobias in America are Public Speaking and Death, in that order. Thus, he quips, "If you're at a funeral, most of the people there would rather be the guy *in the casket* than the one giving the eulogy!"

This tells us something profound: that as much as we fear death, our fear of embarrassment—our self-consciousness—is so great we'd rather die than face the *possibility* of public ridicule. That our social phobia has actually overtaken our survival instinct!

Before we take a closer look at our fear of death, let's look at our fear of public humiliation. Granted if we are to succeed in life it is important to know what other people think of us. This is especially true on the job, where our failure to understand how we're perceived can lead to all kinds of problems, from being turned down for a promotion for not kissing up to the boss, to being fired for sexual harassment for kissing what we're not supposed to.

But for most of us, our self-consciousness goes beyond practical assessment to borderline obsession. We fail to see that, while others may judge us by our words, our deeds and our clothes, most of the time when we're thinking that they're thinking of us, they're actually busy worrying about what *we're* thinking of *them*. Our mistake lies in comparing other folks' outsides to our own neurotic insides—a mistake encouraged by society. A society which tells us it's vitally important to be liked by strangers so we'll run out and buy stuff to keep up with the Joneses and Kardashians—as if the approval of outsiders were a better gauge of our worth than what our own family thinks of us. And so we drive ourselves and our kids (whose behavior reflects on us, after all) insane for the sake of "our image."

In his masterful work *The Untethered Soul*, Michael Singer points out that this is our survival instinct gone haywire. That the same fight or flight instinct that helped save us from saber-toothed tigers has now been focused on defending our self-concepts instead of our lives. That while most of us no longer are without the necessities of food, water, shelter and clothing, we've come to put all our energies into defending our image. That is, we are so concerned about "losing face" that we panic at the thought of uncomfortable social interactions.

Singer argues that we have mistreated our mind by giving it an incomprehensible task—one that has led to the chronic anxiety we face today. That we've told our mind that we want everyone to like us, to make everything we say pleasing to everyone. And that our mind, which, after all is programmed by us, has foolishly agreed to put all of its energy into this impossible task, with the result being that we react to even the smallest perceived slight. Singer says this is unhealthy and unnecessary, as we are all living on a planet spinning around in the middle of outer space and we're worried about stuff that is so inconsequential it's absurd. He points out that our hypersensitivity is a form of suffering that we don't even realize because it's considered "normal" in today's society, where we are constantly worrying about how others see us.

The Importance Of Keeping Up Appearances

One way to see how much importance we place on appearances is to look at what we'll do to look younger. We dye our hair, our beards, our mustaches. We transplant hair from one body part to another. We buy products that promise to grow hair and put them on our scalp no matter how bad they stink.

And when that doesn't work, we comb the 6 and a 1/2 strands we *do* have over our bald pate as if no one can see through the gaps between them—then drive around in Corvettes trying to pick up twenty-somethings with daddy issues.

Women have it even worse, as Society has made a multi-billion dollar industry out of making them look like the twenty-somethings we older men are chasing in our Vettes. Women are told to buy all kinds of lotions to keep their skin from aging. To get cosmetic surgery to tighten up what nature made sag. To starve themselves so they look like younger, skinnier supermodels. To color their hair because they're "worth it."

While some cultures venerate the elderly, our culture worships youth and banishes the old to nursing homes. That's partly because we are selfish. It's also because old people remind us of the Ten Thousand Pound Elephant in the room: Death.

The Fear Of Death: A Cultural Obsession

The great American comedian Woody Allen once said: "I don't want to achieve immortality through my work; I want to achieve immortality through not dying. I don't want to live on in the hearts of my countrymen; I want to live on in my apartment.

That we gods and goddesses will one day cease to exist is so threatening that we have developed a host of ways to keep death at bay. These include denial (when was the last time you saw a dead body?), modern medicine, the diversions created by our multi-billion dollar entertainment industry, and, ironically, arming ourselves to the teeth (we live in a country where 30,000 American civilians die of gun violence annually while our country spends more on defense than the next 9 nations *combined*).* Clearly we as a culture find death VERY disturbing.

Why is this so? In addition to butting heads with our survival instinct, death reminds us that the world does not revolve around us. That we are not gods and goddesses after all. That we are definitely <u>not</u> in control—not only of the minor things we *think* we control, but of our very existence. That none of us can guarantee we will survive the next day, the next hour, the next *second*.

This flies in the face of modern civilization's underlying myth that *we* are in control of our lives. It hits us below the belt as it points to the ultimate futility of our attempts to control Nature rather than seek our place in Her.

Like it or not, modern man is a control freak. Our military, technological, medical and architectural advances can be seen as attempts to control our environment. Physically we've dominated the planet like no species before, building houses that protect us from the weather, with central heating and air conditioning to control the temperature. We've erected huge concrete jungles and sprawling suburbs with paved roads that allow us to travel long distances quickly, driving our natural predators to the brink of extinction.

Yet as we've seen, despite all our modern advances, we aren't happier. Yes, we have more creature comforts than kings. And modern technology has allowed many of us to live like gods, while modern medicine has cured many of our worst diseases and helped us live longer lives. Yet to whatever degree we've mastered our physical ailments, the ailments of the soul still haunt us.

Consider: Every year Americans smoke over 215,000,000,000 cigarettes, spend an estimated $167,000,000,000 on illegal drugs, $260,000,000,000 on prescription drugs and another $200,000,000,000 on alcohol. In addition to the 40 million of us who suffer from anxiety,

---

* While I abhor violence, Russia's invasion of Ukraine has made me thankful for our military as a deterrent to more war-like nations.

another 15 million suffer from major depression, leading to 1.1 million suicide attempts, resulting in over 30,000 deaths. Worldwide this translates to 5.7 trillion cigarettes smoked, almost $300 billion spent on illegal drugs, $1.6 trillion on prescription drugs and another $1.3 trillion spent on alcohol. And the global statistics for anxiety and depression are also shocking. In addition to the previously mentioned statistic of 284 million sufferers of anxiety, another 264 million suffer from major depression resulting in 800,000 people dying from suicide.*

While so much misery may be cause for despair, there is a solution.

Humility To The Rescue

If Consumerism is to blame for making us so selfish and self-conscious (and all the misery that comes from these twin demons), humility is the antidote, as it attacks the root cause of both of these self-diseases: The pre-Copernican notion that the world revolves around us.

As you'll recall from world history class, Nicolas Copernicus broke the news that the Earth revolves around the Sun (and not the other way around) back in 1616 when he published the book *On the Revolutions of the Heavenly Spheres.*

This news was not well received by the Catholic Church, who banned it for the next two centuries. Yet today not even the Taliban would argue that the Sun revolves around the Earth. Still, when it comes to how we live our lives, we act as if Copernicus was a dolt, ignoring a lesson so obvious it screams: "If the Sun does not revolve around the Earth, THE WORLD DOES NOT REVOLVE AROUND US!"

The Good News: Humility Can Be Learned

Of course not everyone lacks humility. As mentioned in the introduction, Alcoholics Anonymous is all about humility. And while this book

---

* The statistics in the preceding paragraph are pre-COVID. I have chosen to keep them the same as are in the previously published audiobook version so you would know that they are not exaggerated by the pandemic.

isn't a 12-step program, to call it A.A. for the self-aholic would not be farfetched. What's more, you probably know many people who've grown in humility over time, including yourself. Perhaps you, too, had a mother who likes to remind you of the arrogant and self-centered things you did as a teenager. And while you can take decades to learn the humility lessons life has to teach you, reading this book and practicing humility is a quicker, easier path than learning through humiliation alone.

That said, deepening our humility takes time and effort. As you read the paths that help you attain humility, I suggest that you revisit those that help you most, internalizing their truths by reviewing them frequently. Developing humility is a daily process, and the more humility you develop, the happier you will be. Still, it is wise to temper our expectations with the following quote from A.A. co-founder Bill Wilson from his groundbreaking work, *Twelve Steps and Twelve Traditions*:

> "To get completely away from our aversion to the idea of being humble, to gain a vision of humility as the avenue to true freedom of the human spirit, to be willing to work for humility as something to be desired for itself, takes most of us a long, long time. *A whole lifetime geared to self-centeredness cannot be set in reverse all at once.*"

This is especially true for those of us living in a society that is constantly bombarding us with anti-humility messages. Telling us the importance of getting rather than giving and the need to keep up with the Joneses and the Kardashians.

Way back in 1953, in *Twelve Steps and Twelve Traditions* Wilson wrote:

> "Humility, as a word and as an ideal, has a very bad time of it in our world. Not only is the idea misunderstood; the word itself is often intensely disliked...Much of the everyday talk we hear, and a great deal of what we read, highlights man's pride in his own achievements..."

Now as we explore the paths to humility that are the meat of this book, let us start the journey of putting ourselves in proper perspective. In so doing let us resurrect "humility" from the mire and lift it to the exalted position St. Augustine put it when he wrote: *"Should you ask me: What is the first thing in religion? I should reply: the first, second and third thing therein is humility."*

Or as this writer might put it, "Should you ask me: What is the most important quality for happiness? I should reply: The first, second and third thing therein is humility."

THE PATHS TO HUMILITY

Putting Ourselves In Proper Perspective

"We had started to get perspective on ourselves,
which is another way of saying we were gaining humility."

— FROM "AA's" *Twelve Steps and Twelve Traditions*

There are three keys to putting ourselves in perspective. We should: 1) not think too highly of ourselves, 2) not think too low of ourselves and 3) not think of ourselves too often. As C.S. Lewis famously wrote: "Humility is not thinking less of yourself, it's thinking about yourself less." While it is obvious that humility helps keep us from thinking of ourselves too highly or too often, it also inspires a healthy self-respect. When we are thinking about ourselves from a place of humility, we realize that, like everything else in the universe, we too have a vital role to play.

A.A. has the 12 steps. *It's* Not *all About You!* has 70 paths.

Paths That Help Us
Not Think Too Highly Of Ourselves

Most people think of humility as not thinking too highly of ourselves. While there are many other aspects to humility, let us start here. The paths in this section are specifically designed to help us not think too highly of ourselves. These paths combat the selfishness and fear that come with being puffed up and therefore vulnerable to being taken down from our lofty perch.

I've divided this section into three subsections: A) How We Relate to Others, B) How We Relate to Ourselves, and C) How We Relate to Life In General. That said, it is humbling to admit, but nonetheless true, that the sections and subsections in *It's Not all About You!* represent my best attempt to structure the book and are not etched in stone.

How We Relate To Others

THE 16 PATHS IN THIS SUBSECTION WILL MAKE YOU A BETTER PERSON. Simple as that. They will make you more popular with others who will want to help you and be around you as your compassion for them grows. Not only will walking these paths make you less selfish, they will make you less self-conscious, reducing anxiety and depression. The paths in this section are particularly useful for helping you put away any angry feelings you have towards others.

The Path Of Recognizing It's Not All About You

As philosopher/guitarist Jimi Hendrix once said: "I used to live in a room full of mirrors, all I could see was me. Then I take my Spirit and I smash my mirrors. Now the whole world is there for me to see!"

The world does not revolve around us. We are not the center of the universe. No matter what our mothers told us when we were little.

While this may seem harsh to our narcissistic ears, it is actually quite freeing. Virtually all of us moderns suffer from an unhealthy level of self-consciousness caused by worrying too much about ourselves and what other people think of us. This is what the Buddha meant when he said that life was suffering.

This anxiety comes largely from our fears about upcoming events and how we're being perceived by others for what we've done in the past or are doing in the present. Most of the paths to humility that help lower anxiety have to do with recognizing it's not all about you.

Depression comes from thinking about how bad life has been in the past, is right now, or will be in the future. As a Licensed Clinical Social Worker, I recognize that clinical depression is often helped by medication and talk therapy. And while many of the paths to humility that help fight depression are found in upcoming books on accepting what you don't like about life and being grateful for everything you do like, putting yourself in perspective and taking your focus off yourself eases depression as well as anxiety.

Once we realize we are not the center of the universe, we are free to enjoy the wonder of it all. Life is then seen as the great gift it is. Something to be cherished and shared with friends and family. For those of us who have a relationship with our Higher Power, knowing that we are able to have a relationship with the Creator of such a vast and mysterious universe fills us with awe and gratitude. Those who do not know or believe in God can think about the role we humans play as the pinnacle of evolution on a planet in an unimaginably large cosmos. When we accept our place in the universe, we feel grateful for the part that God/evolution has chosen us to play in creation.

Removing ourselves from the center of the universe takes a great weight off our shoulders, and we are free to go through our days without having to make Life fit into our own personal agenda. Free to allow ourselves to experience the world without trying to protect ourselves from the natural flow of events.

Now we'll conclude this path, as we will all of the other 69 paths, with an Exercise.

Exercise: Reflect on what ways you are making life all about you. How could you remind yourself that, while you have an important role to play in other people's lives, you are not the center of their universe?

Recognizing Others Are "Other Me's"

"An ordinary and external demon can cause harm, but it is temporary; while the internal demon causes permanent damage... The innermost demon, the one anchored most deeply within us, is the notion of a separate self, the greediness of "me." [emphasis added]

— Dalai Lama, *Essential Teachings*

At first blush, thinking of ourselves makes perfect sense. We look out at the world around us through our own individual pair of eyes. *We* are the ones who hurt when our bodies are in pain. It is *our* stomach that gets hungry when we haven't had enough to eat. *Our* libido that gets excited when we see someone we find attractive. We each have our own history. Our own likes. Our own dislikes. We have our own responsibilities, our own liabilities, our own blessings and trials. In short, we have our own consciousness tied to a single body that is born, grows older and ultimately dies.

But looked at from a different perspective, *other people can be seen to be the same consciousness that just happens to have a different history.* In short, other people are "other me's." No, we don't all think alike, and part of putting yourself in perspective is recognizing and respecting other people's differences. For not only have we each been shaped by our own unique histories on planet Earth, we come to life with different genetic capabilities. When you think about someone whose behavior offends you, remember that, like it or not, if you had been given the same DNA, had the exact same upbringing and experienced everything they had experienced up to this point as the result of their behavior, you too would, in all likelihood, be making the same bad choices they are making.* Recognizing this leads to compassion—a quality the Dalai Lama says is the key to happiness.

---

* Although a person might argue that your soul, being more highly evolved, would not have chosen that person's incarnation—a philosophical discussion for another time.

Knowing this, we see that, if we were in their shoes and had their DNA, we too could have been a Nelson Mandela, an Abraham Lincoln, a Martin Luther King, a Mother Teresa, a Moses, a Buddha, a Muhammed, a Yogananda—or simply a person in our life who we admire. This should fill us with a sense of awe at our own possibilities.

On the flipside, given the same life history and DNA of those we abhor, we are all capable of doing the most despicable things. As Zora Neale Hurston put it so eloquently in her autobiography *Dust Tracks on a Road*:

> "You who play the zig-zag lightning of power over the world, with the grumbling thunder in your wake, think kindly of those who walk in the dust. And you who walk in humble places, think kindly too, of others. There has been no proof in the world so far that you would be less arrogant if you held the lever of power in your hands."

Recognizing this brings compassion for our enemies, as it shows us that those who we revile because they have wronged us have treated us the same way we would have treated ourselves if we had been in their shoes. This helps cure resentment and unforgiveness.

Seeing others as other "me's" also means recognizing that they are as self-absorbed as we are. That when we walk into a room they are more concerned with how they're being perceived than they are judging us— something we'll get to in Section IV on paths that help us think about ourselves less.

◈

Exercise: Think about how other people—especially any you consider your "enemies"—are really other "you's" in different bodies. Reflect on the fact that if you were in their shoes, you would likely be making the same bad choices they are making.

The Path Of Lowering Our Expectations
Of What Others Can Do For Us

One path to humility that will make you much happier with other people is to stop expecting too much from them.

Whether or not you believe that human beings are sinful by nature, we can all agree that all of us are imperfect at best and downright nasty at times.

I find that having too high of an expectation of others often gets in the way of appreciating and accepting them for who they are. Having overly high expectations causes me to focus on the ways in which they fail to meet my needs.

Lowering our expectations of others helps us to be humbly grateful for the positive things they bring to the relationship. I recently went on a road trip with my father and my son around New Year's. We'd done the same trip the year before and I'd been disappointed in how some of my relatives had treated me. This time, I vowed to lower my expectations. It helped. Somewhat. I still am sensitive about the way some of my relatives come at me with subtle challenges and put downs, but I'm re-reading this section of the book as I'm writing this to help me accept their behavior without becoming aggressive or negative myself.

After all, if I can't benefit from my writing and grow in humility, how can I ask others to do the same?

༄

Exercise: The next time you attend a social event with people that make you uneasy, lower your expectations.

The Path Of Having Compassion For Others

Compassion is caring about others. The Dalai Lama says it is the key to happiness. One reason I agree with him is that the more judgmental we are of others (and therefore less compassionate towards them), the more judgmental we tend to be of ourselves. This psychological truth is bolstered by the notion of karma, which says that the universe will reward us for our deeds—a notion that finds expression in the Bible which says we will "reap what [we] sow."

But compassion is not merely about not judging others; it involves helping others as well. When we stop and think about how other people are other "me's," we realize that the good we do to others is really helping ourselves. This is especially true when dealing with our so-called enemies. Here we could learn from the examples of the great men and women of compassion.

Nelson Mandela led a peaceful transition from the horrors of apartheid to a country where the White minority and Black majority could live in peace.

This was made possible through Mandela's insistence on forgiving the Afrikaners who put him in prison for 28 years while systematically degrading, murdering and torturing the people he led.

In one of his sermons, Dr. Martin Luther King talks about the importance of not responding to one injustice with another, using the example of not shining your car's brights at someone who fails to dim them for you.

The Dalai Lama goes so far as to say that our enemies are really our best friends, as they point out our flaws in ways that help us grow: "We must consider an adversary as possibly and perhaps definitely our best friend, in a very special way…The guru, the teachings we receive from him, our friends and family—none are as valuable to us as those who disturb us." (*Essential Teachings* p. 48)

In the Sermon on the Mount, Jesus states: "But I say unto you, Love your enemies, bless them that curse you, do good to them that hate you, and pray for them which despitefully use you, and persecute you;" (Matthew 5:44, King James Version)

Jesus backed this up with actions. He let Himself be crucified and said of those who jeered Him as He hung on the cross, "Forgive them Lord, for they know not what they do."

Compassion keeps us from putting ourselves above others. In so doing it helps us not to think too highly of ourselves. This leads to two practical paths: The path of dressing humbly and the path of driving a humble automobile—both of which help us avoid the pitfall of treating people differently based on their positions in society.

❦

Exercise: Practice an act of compassion today, doing something for someone else—one that doesn't benefit you in any way. This could mean giving to charity, or giving a dollar to someone who is selling a newspaper or asking for spare change.

The Path Of Driving A Humble Automobile

Today people like to drive fancy cars. Not only because they are more luxurious but because they are a status symbol. Have you ever looked at other cars and judged the people in them even if you haven't gotten a look at the driver?

If you're like me, when someone cuts you off while driving a Mercedes Benz you think of them as a rich bastard who's in a hurry to get to the yacht club. You might even give them the finger.

Now should that same person cut you off in a thugged-up ride with tinted windows, a booming rap bass line and a license plate that says "Guilty1," (an actual description of the car owned by one of my Caucasian clients)—you'd be wise to keep all your fingers on the steering wheel.

Driving a more humble automobile than you can afford is a path to humility. I read about a German billionaire who drove a Ford Focus, and I'm always impressed by someone with a lofty title who drives a modest vehicle. A related path is the path of driving humbly, something we'll discuss in the section on "hurry."

❧

Exercise: Buy a cheap car.

PATH TO HUMILITY #6

The Path Of Dressing Humbly

The path of dressing humbly is particularly hard for those of us who think we're sexy. As the ZZ Top song goes, "Every girl's crazy 'bout a sharp dressed man." And it's true. I find that when I walk around wearing a suit, women treat me differently than if I'm wearing, say, coffee-stained sweatpants.

Although the truth was that I dressed sharp because my wife insisted on it, my co-workers at the State of Connecticut's Department of Mental Health and Addiction Services felt I wore the clothes I did because I was a hoighty-toighty LCSW (that is, Licensed Clinical Social Worker). At least that was what some of the Recovery Pathways workers thought. You see, the RP workers were mostly social workers who were unable to pass the social work licensing exam. One of those RP workers was Shamus McNasty (not his real name), a large, red-bearded Irishman who prided himself on his power as a union rep. I once heard him on the phone boasting that "I treats people well who treats me well." A man who faked a seizure to avoid getting in trouble for parking illegally—then bragged about it at work. A paragon of arrogance who once invited himself to co-lead my spirituality groups without being asked.

Anyway, this same Shamus attended a presentation I gave on humility, where he noted, quite appropriately, that when we're pointing our fingers at someone else we've got three fingers pointing back at ourselves. I was impressed. Perhaps he wasn't such a bad soul after all. Then right after the presentation was over, he came up to me and slammed the LCSWs for being a bunch of arrogant SOB's—apparently blind to the fact that he was doing the exact same thing he complained about fifteen minutes before!

To his credit, Shamus never wore snazzy threads. He viewed himself as a blue-collar man, and dressed accordingly. Others who follow the practice of dressing humbly are monks like the Dalai Lama who wear the same robe every day. This act of humility reflects their focus on their inner transformation.

Exercise: Try dressing down for a day. Notice how this affects your humility.

The Path Of Treating People
Like People And Not By Their Titles

While I hate to admit it, I have sometimes treated people differently based on their social position. As Shamus would be quick to tell you, I was guilty of thinking that I, as a Licensed Clinical Social Worker with three masters degrees and an Ivy league BA, was better than the aforementioned RP workers. Although I am currently my own boss as a psychotherapist in private practice, when I was working with the State of Connecticut, I was keenly aware of the social hierarchy and was guilty of treating "underlings" (RP workers) differently than the supervisors and psychiatrists who were my "superiors." This can be countered by The Path of Treating People Like People.

Now humans are social animals, and we are constantly jockeying for position in the social hierarchy. Anthropologist Desmond Morris states that much of the angst modern mankind feels is due to what he calls "frustrated ladder climbing." What we call the "pecking order." Morris points out that our brains are hard-wired to deal with groups of forty or so individuals, as we were hunter-gatherers who lived in small tribes for much longer than we've been living in what he calls "supertribes," or the nation-states that we live in today. Here to make it to the top of the social ladder you have to be one in millions rather than one in forty. And even the lowliest in the small tribe was a significant $1/40^{th}$ of the whole. Far more significant than the 1 millionth in a Supertribe.

My dad, who is a world-renowned scientist, likes to wear a janitor's sweater he bought from one of the maintenance men at Yale. He wears it to suggest that he is just people too. When I told him that I thought he was a good person because he doesn't treat people based on their social positions, he didn't understand me at first. Then, after pausing for a moment, he said "Oh, you mean I treat people like they are people."

I'm also reminded of my father's former girlfriend who graduated from Harvard but told people she was from Boston College. A lie, yes, but a humble one.

Exercise: Remind yourself that we are all human beings no matter what our position in society. Make a conscious effort to treat each individual you meet today with the respect they deserve regardless of their title or lack thereof.

The Five Paths Of Not Judging Others

THE PATH OF NOT JUDGING OTHERS IS REALLY A CLUSTER OF PATHS. FIRST comes recognizing the difference between judging and evaluating. This is followed by several paths that help us recognize we have no business judging others.

Recognizing The Difference
Between Judging And Evaluating

There is nothing wrong with evaluating others. We need to evaluate others to know who to trust and believe. That's different than being judgmental. Condemning others in our minds. Deeming them less worthy than ourselves.

We judge others because we are insecure and we want to make ourselves feel superior. Judging is an act of pride.

If we are honest with ourselves, we see that we are constantly judging others, placing them below ourselves in some form or fashion. We judge others at work, in our families, in church. We may do this in our heads or go a step further and spread our ideas through gossip or even openly disrespecting the person we have judged.

Exercise: Think about those people who you have some complaint about. Then remind yourself that they are "other me's" and avoid the temptation to judge them.

The First Reason To Stop Judging:
The Path Of Recognizing
We Don't Know Enough About Them

The first reason we shouldn't judge others is that we don't know enough about them. We only see the outside, not what's going on inside. We don't know what their lives are like when we're not with them. We don't know how they were raised. The trials they've been through. The potential they have.

We are all unique, and it takes all different parts to make up the body of humanity. For us to criticize others because they don't do things exactly the way we would is like your foot complaining that your hand is worthless because you can't walk on it. Just because people do things differently than you'd like doesn't make them wrong. In fact, we all benefit from the different gifts we possess. As mentioned before, it's our ability to share those gifts with each other that makes humans so successful. If everyone was just like you, the human race would have died out long ago, as it takes a man and a woman to procreate. And we all know how different men and women are! As the French say, "Vive la Difference!"

When we judge others, we are looking at the outward actions without knowing what's going on inside the person's heart. That's why we excuse ourselves based on our situations, but attribute others' miscues to character defects. If we're speeding, it's because we're in a hurry to get somewhere. If it's someone else, it's because they're a jerk.

As we'll explore in the next section, we don't even know enough about OURSELVES to judge ourselves fairly. We don't know our potential or remember what it was like in those formative years before we can remember—formative years psychologists say were crucial to our development. And if we can't even judge ourselves, how on Earth can we judge others?

❦

Exercise: As you are tempted to judge others throughout the course of your day, remind yourself that you don't know enough about that person to judge him or her.

The Second Reason To Stop Judging:
The Path Of Recognizing We Do
The Same Things As Those We Judge

I had a client at the Department of Mental Health and Addiction Services, a woman who was complaining about her wife. "All she does is take, take, take," she said. "And she takes no responsibility for any of her actions. Everything that happens to her is someone else's fault." When I gently suggested that sometimes the things we despise in others are the same things we do ourselves, she didn't make the connection *at all*. What I really wanted to say was, "Look, you do the exact same things you complain your wife is doing! Take, take, take but taking NO responsibility for your own actions? That's a perfect description of *you*!" But I didn't say that because it would have been unprofessional.

I personally have a problem with a certain former basketball player who I consider to be one of the most arrogant people on the planet. That said, I realize that I wouldn't have a problem with said player's arrogance if I didn't have some arrogance of my own.

Likewise, I have a big problem with bullies. As a child I was born with a birth defect that gave me a droopy eyelid. Now children can be cruel.

Especially when they see another who is "different" from them. And when that child is relatively frail and intelligent and raised not to defend himself, not to mention a little bit arrogant, well... that is a recipe for disaster.

I got picked on a lot in grade school and junior high, but it never occurred to me that I used to bully others until I ran into my old friend Robert Grossman when I was in my thirties. Robbie and I had been best friends as children. But when Robbie saw me as an adult, he simply sneered at me and said "Robbie, get the big net!" Then he turned his back and walked away.

You see, Robbie and I used to hang out on a small dock trying to catch little fish or crabs. For some reason we always seemed to bring only the little net. Invariably I would see something that called for "the big net" and, instead of going to get it myself, I would yell "Robbie, get the big net!" And Robbie would run off to fetch it for me.

The Bible talks about the mistake of trying to pull a splinter out of your brother's eye when there is a beam in your own. The extent to which someone else's arrogance bothers you only shows your own lack of humility.

Being non-judgmental is one key to developing humility. When we stop judging others, we stop being as critical of ourselves. How many of you know that IT'S OK TO MAKE MISTAKES?

❧

Exercise: When someone's behavior irritates you today, ask yourself how you may be guilty of the same thing. Then forgive them and let the ill-effects of their behavior evaporate like water off a duck's back.

The Third Reason To Stop Judging:
The Path Of Recognizing Others May Be
Living Up To Their Potential More Than We Are

As we discussed before, it's clear that we shouldn't judge others because we don't know enough about them to judge fairly. But what if we are right?

What if that other person is not at our level spiritually. That they aren't as mature as us? We STILL shouldn't judge them! Why? Because, for all we know, they are living up to their potential more than we are.

Let's say we're a "7" when it comes to our humility and they're a "4." We could look down on them, but then we would fall to a "6." For surely we would be more humble if we didn't judge them. Besides, given who they are and what they've been exposed to, a "4" could be OVER achieving for that individual and a "7" could be UNDER achieving for you. Maybe they *should* be a "2" and you *should* be a "9." The point is, just because you're more advanced than someone else doesn't mean you're living up to your potential more than they are.

Take myself for example. While I might be tempted to think that I'm doing pretty well spiritually, I have to recognize all the benefits I've had. I was blessed with good genes and a stable, nurturing home environment. In college my parents encouraged me to follow my dreams, and my grandfather was so rich I felt free to major in Eastern Religion at Columbia University in the belief (sadly mistaken) that I'd never have to worry about money. Moreover, the reason I got into the Ivy league college in the first place was that the pool of applicants had been cut in half because Columbia did not accept women undergrads back in 1980 (an unfortunate truth I only discovered after arriving on campus, as they somehow failed to highlight it on their application literature). Not to mention all of the spiritual blessings I've been blessed with. It's written in the five books of Moses (the first five books of the Bible) that Moses was the humblest man on Earth. What's interesting is that it is said that Moses *wrote* those five books. So it seems Moses wrote that he was the humblest man on Earth! The explanation? That Moses realized someone else who'd had Moses' gifts could have been a better Moses than Moses was.

Exercise: Look at the people who you judge as being spiritually immature. Now remember that those same people 1) may be more mature than you think, and 2) may be living up to their potential more than you—even if you are right about them being less mature than you are.

The Fourth Reason To Stop Judging:
The Path Of Recognizing That We Shouldn't Judge Others Because We Don't Want To Be Judged

We shouldn't judge others harshly because we don't want to be judged harshly, either by others, ourselves or God.

It's a psychological truth that the harsher we judge others, the harsher we tend to judge ourselves. The more you use that little voice inside your head to criticize others, the more harshly that little voice inside your head will judge you.

Likewise, it is also true that the more you go around judging others, the more others will find fault with you. This is just a variation on the theme of karma, the universal law that everything you do comes back to you.

But beyond being judged by ourselves and others, none of us wants to face judgment when we die. That's because we'd all be found guilty. In the Sermon on the Mount, Jesus made it plain that even to think badly of others was a sin. And Jesus also points out that breaking one part of the law makes us guilty of breaking the whole Law. If you get pulled over for speeding, it won't do you any good to say "Well, officer, I haven't murdered anyone."*

✧

Exercise: Whenever you are tempted to judge someone, remind yourself that you don't want to be judged harshly and that the less you judge others, the less you will be judged.

---

*That said, it might help to ask him if he's offering to sell you tickets to the State Trooper's ball. Funny story. An attractive woman gets pulled over by a state trooper and tells him "I know, you want to sell me two tickets to that state trooper's ball." To which the trooper replies "Lady, state troopers don't have balls." When the trooper realizes how his comment could be taken, he is so embarrassed he gets back in his cruiser and drives away.

The Path Of Forgiving Others

This path starts with the following quote from the book *Humility* by
Peter Wagner: "Humility is a willingness to be underestimated or
slighted and feel no resentment."

If not judging others is critical to our walk with humility, so is forgiveness. When we refuse to forgive someone, we are not only judging
them, we are allowing them to torment us. Forgiveness is a path to
humility because we no longer hold on to the pride that was hurt when
we were wronged by our "enemy."

Nelson Mandela insisted on forgiving the white Afrikaners who
murdered and tortured his people and locked him in prison for 28 years.

A concentration camp victim in Nazi Germany left the following
message behind: "O Lord, Remember not only the men and women of
good will but all those of ill will. But do not remember all the suffering
they have inflicted upon us; remember the fruits we have bought thanks
to this suffering—our comradeship, our loyalty, our humility, our courage, our generosity, the greatness of heart which has grown out of all
this; and when they come to judgment, let all the fruits we have borne
be their forgiveness."

And then there's Jesus. If he could forgive the people who mocked
Him while crucifying Him, who are we to be judging? When Jesus was
dying on the Cross He didn't say "Lord, reward them according to their
works" or "Give them all hemorrhoids the size of golf balls."*

---

* This brings to mind the story in the little-known "Gospel According to Daniel Cohen"
where Jesus and Moses went golfing. Moses asks Jesus "What club are you going to use
here?" To which Jesus replies "Tiger Woods would use a 9 iron." Jesus then uses the 9
iron and, because He's not as good a golfer as Tiger Woods, proceeds to leave it short.
This is repeated several times, with the last time ending with Jesus hitting the ball into
the water. When He goes walking on the water to retrieve his ball, another golfer shouts
out "Who does that guy think he is, Jesus Christ?" to which Moses replies "No, Tiger
Woods!" This illustrates two important points: 1) that Jesus' lack of humility in this
instance caused him to be humiliated by Moses; and 2) that God Himself has a sense of
humor for allowing me to make His Son Jesus the butt of one of my jokes!

If Nelson Mandela could forgive the White South Africans for killing and torturing his brothers, if the concentration camp victim could forgive the Nazis who mistreated and murdered her comrades, if Jesus could forgive those who were crucifying Him, who are we not to forgive somebody who said or did something we don't like?

The challenge is to love our enemies. This is not for THEIR good, but for OURS. Unless you are actively hurting your enemy, all of your anger at them is only hurting you. As a Buddhist saying goes, hating another person is like drinking poison and expecting the other person to get sick. Or, as I've heard it said in A.A., holding a grudge is like peeing on yourself and expecting the other person to get wet. When you love and pray for your enemies, it takes the anger and resentment out of you, and you don't come at the person from a negative state of mind. It gives you inner peace. The kind of peace that is priceless.

If it's a law of the universe that everything you do comes back to you, don't you want to put a little forgiveness out there? After all, you may be clicking on all cylinders today, but the day will come when you will slip and you will want someone to forgive you.

Exercise: Think of all the people in your life who you consider "enemies." Then forgive them and pray for them as if they were your closest friends, remembering the example of Nelson Mandela, the concentration camp victim, and Jesus on the cross. (If you don't believe in prayer, wish them well.)

The Path Of Going Beyond Forgiveness And Responding To Mistreatment With Humble Love

"Of some thoughts one stands perplexed—especially at the sight of men's sin—and wonders whether one should use force or humble love. Always decide to use humble love. If you resolve on that, once and for all, you may subdue the whole world. Loving humility is marvelously strong, and strongest of all things, and there is nothing else like it."

— Fyodor Dostoyevsky, Russian novelist

In the preceding quotation, Dostoyevsky is talking about the awesome power of turning the other cheek when one is mistreated. Martin Luther King talks about the same issue in one of his sermons, when he describes riding down a highway with a friend of his at the wheel. That night, Dr. King says, the drivers in the oncoming traffic were being impolite and were shining their brights in their eyes. When Dr. King's friend declared that he was going to shine his brights back on them, Dr. King responded "No, you mustn't do that!" His point? Retaliation leads to a cycle of escalating violence.

Why should you show "humble love" to someone who has been unkind to you?

First, being nice has a wonderful effect on people. Who knows what that person is going through? If they are acting mean, it is a sure sign that they aren't happy. Rather than wanting to get even with the person, we should feel sorry for them and want to lift them up. When we do this, we help create a happier world.

This is easier said than done, for our society often mistakes humility for weakness. And there is the fear that if we don't stand up for ourselves, we will invite further humiliation. This exaggerated need for self-defense often stems from childhood trauma. Maybe we were picked on in school or abused by our siblings or parents when we couldn't defend ourselves and now feel we must stand up for ourselves at every turn.

I've observed that many of us are sensitive to criticism of any kind—at least I know I am. And this sensitivity comes from having an exaggerated sense of self-importance. When I get my feelings hurt, I like to remind myself of Peter Wagner's quote about humility being "a willingness to be underestimated or slighted and feel no resentment." While I don't claim to be even close to there yet, I am working on it.

I recently traveled across country and wound up forgetting to bring one of my medications. When I called my doctor's office to request that they call it in to the pharmacy in Indiana, the prescriber on call was livid that I had called on the Sunday before Christmas.

She proceeded to humiliate me in no uncertain terms, telling me that I was a horrible person for having inconvenienced her. Her tone was rude and accusatory. She ended the conversation by telling me that I'd "better not do this again." As if I made a habit of doing so. That I was a 56-year-old man who'd NEVER had this problem in the past made no difference to her. She just wanted to make me feel bad for forcing her to make a phone call she didn't want to make.

I ended the phone call with her by saying "Have a blessed day." Then I spent the next few moments thinking about how I would get her fired for her lack of compassion. I justified my thinking by pointing out that she probably deserved to be canned and that I shouldn't allow her to go unpunished as she might treat others this way if I don't speak out. Then I reminded myself that this was not the path God had laid out for me. So instead, I resolved to send her a letter, which I ultimately decided not to write.

❧

Exercise: The next time someone does something you don't like, respond with kindness. If it doesn't change the other person, at least you can go on with your life feeling good about yourself.

The Path Of Not Feeling Superior
Because Of Our Political Or Religious Beliefs

The other day I opened up a Facebook page from a dear old friend. Right there in front of me was a right-wing political blurb that cried foul, suggesting voter fraud in the election of Barak Obama in 2012, as all 190,000 plus voters in a single congressional district in Philadelphia voted for Obama. It took me back for a second, as I get most of my news from National Public Radio and MSNBC, both of which suggest that "voter fraud" in American elections is extremely rare and merely a smoke screen aimed at denying voter rights to blacks and other minorities who tend to vote Democratic. What's more, as my brother Avrum pointed out, the fact that there was a district made up *entirely* of Obama voters spoke more to the success of Republican gerrymandering than Democratic fraud.*

This got me thinking that feeling superior because of my political beliefs was not at all in keeping with the path of humility. After all, thinking our way is the only right way to think hardly qualifies as humble. This led me to ponder an even deeper conceit. That of my religious beliefs. And while I have not been shy in this book about my religious beliefs, I recognize that others hold different beliefs which may well be more correct than my own.

Certainly we have a right, even a duty, to have our own political and religious beliefs. Our political beliefs speak to how we think we should treat one another, while our religious beliefs speak to how we should

---

* For those unfamiliar with the term, gerrymandering is the process whereby one political party's state legislature draws out voting districts in such a way that almost all of the voters in a particular district are from the opposition's party, keeping those voters from influencing races in other, closer, congressional districts. A shameful practice that has been done by both democrats and republicans.

treat our relationship to our Higher Power. And we like to believe that our beliefs are right, which means others' beliefs are "wrong."

My father is an atheist. He is also mad at God. (When I point out that you can't be mad at a God you don't believe in, I get nowhere). Dad is fond of pointing out how much blood has been shed in the name of religion. That while currently much of that comes from Muslim extremists, Christians were responsible for the Inquisition and The Crusades, and that American Christians and Jews both owned slaves. That even Hitler's Third Reich had Christian Support, as 1/3rd of Germans were Catholic and 2/3rds Protestant.

While Dad will point out all the evil done by religious folk, I would counter that much good has been done by them as well, and that for all we know it is the prayers of the saints that are keeping God Almighty from wiping the human race off of the face of the Earth.

Who's right? No one can say for sure.

Exercise: Talk to someone of another religious faith about their beliefs, read one of their holy books or visit one of their holy places.

A Personal Note On
How My Own Religious Path Makes It
Easy To Accept Other Faith Traditions

While it is relatively easy for me to say that my religious beliefs are not the only spiritual path, it is clearly much more difficult for some who have only known one faith tradition all of their lives. For although I am a pastor in a Christian church, I am not your typical Christian.

While I am deeply committed to the faith, and believe that Jesus died on a Cross so I could be forgiven for my sins—a belief I've held since 1993 when I first started my walk with Christ—I wasn't born a Christian. In fact, I was raised as a secular Jew by parents who did not believe in God. What's more, I didn't come directly from Jewish atheism to Christianity, but took the scenic route, having had a Spiritual awakening as a freshman in college where, consumed by the meaninglessness of an existence that would end with my death, I was given the Gift of a direct experience of God that caused me to realize both His Deity and the fact that I was a Spiritual being who would live on long after Daniel Cohen left his earthly body.

That summer I would have a mystical experience while looking through water droplets on my sunglasses where each drop took on the shape like a shining thumbprint and tears of ecstasy rolled down my cheeks. That this was indeed a spiritual experience was confirmed that fall when I read a Hindu religious text called *The Bagavad Gita* and had the same ecstatic tearing experience. Similar experiences would come when reading Buddhist texts such as *The Platform Sutra of the Sixth Patriarch*, and I soon realized that these sacred texts were designed to get me to this state of enlightenment. This would lead me to become a Zen Buddhist in college where I held the bias that Eastern religions were inherently superior to the "religions of the word" (Judaism, Christianity and Islam), which, in my youthful arrogance I dismissed as unspiritual belief systems designed to tell me how to live my life.

All of this would change in 1993 when I first experienced the Holy Spirit and became a Christian, and then again in 1996 when I had a "second conversion" of sorts—this time to the African American church, where I've been for the last 24 years.

So, while it's easy for me to say that there are many paths to God, I understand how tempting it can be for those who've only known one set of religious beliefs to believe that they are superior to those who hold different beliefs.

The Path Of "I Used To Be Disgusted But Now I Try To Be Amused"

One of my favorite strategies for dealing with difficult people comes from an Elvis Costello song. The line is "I used to be disgusted, and now I try to be amused." That is, instead of getting angry at the negative things people do, try to find something humorous about it. For if you can rise above your anger and see other people's power plays as amusingly immature ways of getting their needs met, you are on your way to a healthier state of mind.

Say your boss goes on a power trip and insists that it's his way or the highway. You can imagine him as a two-year-old having a temper tantrum and screaming "I want it MY way!" This may help you respond more positively, as being disgusted makes you feel superior, while being amused leads to compassion.

What's interesting about this strategy, is that there's a second component to it just in case it doesn't work at first. That is, when we find ourselves stewing about what someone else has done to us and just can't wrap our heads around finding any amusement in it, we can apply the principle to ourselves.

We can look at our inability to forgive and let go of the anger as something about ourselves which we can be amused at instead of being our own worst critic. This helps relieve us of unnecessary guilt.

❧

Exercise: When someone—or something—tempts you to get angry today, remind yourself of the wisdom of Elvis Costello's "I used to be disgusted, and now I try to be amused." If that doesn't work, look at your negative reaction with compassion and try to be amused at the fact that you weren't able to be amused in the first place. If that doesn't work, take a double shot of Jack Daniels (just kidding church folk! ;-).

You may also choose to do what one of my clients did and write down all of the stupid stuff others say and do to you—then go back and read it and see how ridiculous it was. My client said this helped him deal with the hassles of living in a homeless shelter.

SUBSECTION B

How We Relate To Ourselves: (Paths That Help Us To Not Take Ourselves Too Seriously)

IF THE PREVIOUS SECTION HELPS US RELATE TO OTHERS BETTER, THE 5 paths in this section will help us feel more comfortable in our own skins. The paths here are closely related to the paths in Section III, as not taking ourselves too seriously is related to not thinking too low of ourselves.

The Path Of Not Taking
Ourselves Too Seriously

In his excellent book, *The Teachings of Don Juan: A Yaqui Way of Knowledge*, Carlos Castaneda talks about not taking ourselves too seriously. In his book, Don Juan, a Yaqui Indian Wiseman who takes Castaneda under his wing, tells Castaneda that his biggest problem is that he takes himself too seriously, and this makes him "too heavy" to be a Man of Knowledge.

Taking ourselves too seriously is the same mistake Winston made at the beginning of this book, causing me to scream "It's Not All About You Winston!" over and over again. So it's only natural that a path to humility is NOT taking ourselves too seriously.

For those who were paying close attention, the second part of the "I used to be disgusted" technique actually belongs in the section on "How we relate to ourselves." As these paths indicate, not thinking too highly of ourselves is as important to how we relate to ourselves as it is to how we relate to others.

It helps to look at WHY we get disgusted with ourselves. In addition to being a pastor, I am a psychotherapist. As such I've been trained to look at the root causes for our current ways of thinking. Perhaps we had critical parents who we've internalized so that the little voice in our heads is one of judgment rather than that of a compassionate life coach. Or maybe our religious beliefs are based on a judgmental and punitive God. Whatever the reason, it is a lack of humility that is at the root of our self-condemnation.

"How can that be, Oh Great and Mighty Humility Czar?" you ask. "If I'm judging myself harshly, I'm certainly not thinking too highly of myself." Actually, judging yourself harshly is denying your basic humanity. Humans weren't meant to be perfect. If you're judging yourself harshly it's because you think you're supposed to be superhuman. That you are really better than the rest of us—or at least better than the flawed human being you actually are. This leads to The Path of Recognizing You're Only Human.

Exercise: The next time you're disgusted with yourself for something you've done, remind yourself of your humanity and find something amusing in your own bad behavior—or your insistence on being "perfect."

The Path Of Recognizing You're Only Human

While it's been said that "humility is not thinking less of yourself but thinking of yourself less," I would add that sometimes it's both. For me at least, I often find that reminding myself of my flaws helps me humble myself and put myself back in perspective.

To that end I'd like to invite you to take A.A.'s Fearless Moral Inventory.

As you do so, keep in mind that the purpose of this path is not to beat yourself up, but to recognize your humanity (that is, your inability to be perfect), and be okay with it.

Taking A Fearless Moral Inventory

"To those who have made progress in A.A., it ["humility"] amounts to a clear recognition of what and who we really are, followed by a sincere attempt to become what we could be. Therefore, our first practical move toward humility must consist of recognizing our deficiencies. No defect can be corrected unless we clearly see what it is."

—*Twelve Steps and Twelve Traditions*

Recognizing our flaws and owning up to them is a key to humility. I'd like you to take time out now and write down the ways you've wronged God or others (those of you who are being honest may require a lot of paper).

ॐ

My favorite line about our sinfulness comes from a <u>Game of Thrones</u> episode where Lord Varis is trying to build up Tyrion's ego after he smuggled him out of King's Landing. After Varis finishes building him up, Tyrion protests:

"I killed my lover with my bare hands. I shot my father with a cross-bow." he says.

"I never said you were perfect," Varis replies without missing a beat.

ॐ

Recognizing that we are only human requires us to recognize that other people are only human, too. When we stop expecting ourselves to be perfect, we can stop expecting others to be perfect as well. This relates to the path of expecting less and getting more which we'll discuss in Section IV.

The Recognition That We Are All Sinners:
A path especially for my Christian readers

We who call ourselves "Christians" can take this one step farther. Because when it comes right down to it, we Christians have the greatest way to humble ourselves. That's to remind ourselves how OUR sin (your sin, not someone else's) cost Jesus the ultimate price on the cross 2,000 years ago.

If nothing else I've written has made you feel humble, I want you to focus on what Christ did for you on the cross. Note the nails in his wrists and ankles. Think of the tremendous pain he went through as the crowd mocked him. The very sinners who Christ was dying for, jeering him and laughing at his agony. Remember His words "Forgive them Lord, for they know not what they do." Now remember that these words are directed to you personally every time you sin.

While humility is not about beating ourselves up, we as saved Christians need to recognize precisely what sinners we are. Not by making some blanket admission of sin, such as "Oh yes, I'm a sinner because the Bible tells me so." But by getting down and dirty and taking a thoughtful examination of just how we grieve the Holy Spirit who lives within us with our particular sins. Those that we've committed in the past and those that we haven't let go of yet, remembering not only our deeds but our thoughts as well.

Here it's worth reminding ourselves that worry is sin, as it shows a lack of faith in God, who knows all and without Whom nothing happens that was not ordained from the beginning of time.

Exercise: Take a fearless moral inventory of yourself, writing down all of your faults and taking a good hard look at yourself. If you are a Christian, consider your sins and recognize that they were the reason Jesus had to die on the Cross.

The Path Of Self-Deprecating Humor

The heavy weight of our sins can be balanced by a sense of humor. It is humbling not to take ourselves so seriously that we can't laugh at ourselves.

I like to joke that my ego is so large it could have applied for statehood. I also want everyone to refer to me as "The Almighty Humility Czar." (This is actually true—but all of my close friends just call me "Czar.")

People like it when you are able to poke fun at yourself. It takes a healthy ego to recognize one's imperfections. I had a close friend I worked with in the Office of Student Activities when I was a college student. He was a full-fledged adult, a mentor of mine who would make me laugh all the time.

Yet this man who was so sweet to me and everyone else, was merciless when dealing with this one Chinese student.

When I asked him why he was picking on the student, he replied "Because he thinks his s— doesn't stink." That he didn't like the young man because he couldn't laugh at himself.

I think the one thing people miss most when they think about God is His sense of humor. After all, the Bible says we are made in God's image, and laughter is something all healthy adults do. I once heard something on National Public Radio about the importance of play that has stuck with me over the years. What is the thing that children do ten times more than grownups?

Laugh.

The ability to make fun of yourself is an essential path to humility and is part of the path of not taking yourself too seriously. When you can make fun of yourself, you show the world that you're confident enough to laugh at your own foibles. As you will recall from the introduction,

I like to say that my ego is so large that, if it applied for statehood, it would become the fourth largest state in the union right behind Alaska, California and Texas.

For someone who's writing about humility, that's a risky thing to admit. However, it would be more risky—and less accurate—to say that I had attained such a great level of humility that I didn't need to re-read these paths to keep me humble. That I was writing this book because I saw how much everyone else needs it. You know, the kind of thing Shamus McNasty would say.

That said, I am much more humble than I used to be. It's just that that isn't saying much—as we'll see when we get to some of the personal anecdotes in our discussion of the Law of Humility and Humiliation right after path #42.

Exercise: Look back on something you've done in your life that was embarrassing and try to find the humor in it. Better yet, next time the opportunity arises, make fun of yourself in public and notice the reaction you get.

The Path Of Comparing Ourselves
To Those Who Gave More

One way to put your ego in check is to compare yourself to the great men and women of humility who have shaped history for the good of humankind.

Spiritual giants like Jesus, Mohammed, Moses, the Buddha, Gandhi, Mother Teresa, Dr. Martin Luther King, Jr. and the Dalai Lama of Tibet.

Unlike comparing ourselves to those who *got* more (which as we've seen is Consumerism's way of making us feel crummy so we go out and buy stuff), comparing ourselves to those who *gave* more is a powerfully humbling experience that puts our ego in check and challenges us to follow their selfless examples.

Ultimately, however, we can only compare ourselves to who we were in the past. Rabbi Akiva, a famous rabbi who lived around the first century A.D., once said that he didn't fear that when he went before the judgment seat of God, He would ask him why he hadn't done as much as this great rabbi or that one, but only that he hadn't done as well as he could have with the gifts God had given *him*. I, too, share the same fear.

Exercise: Compare yourselves to the Spiritual giants and ask yourself in what small way you could be more like them today.

The Path Of Recognizing
How Little We Know Ourselves

If the first reason we can't judge others is that we don't know enough about them, the same can, to a lesser extent, be said about judging ourselves.

As we discussed in the section on not judging others, you may think you know yourself well, but only God knows everything about why you are who you are. The genetics, the things your mother was going through while you were yet in the womb, the things that happened to you as a child before you were old enough to remember them,* everything we've experienced that we've forgotten—all these things are lost to us.

In his book, *The Untethered Soul*, Michael Singer points out that defining ourselves is actually quite difficult. For example, are we the person who shows up when we are in a bad mood or when things are going well? The self you were when you were 5 years old girl, or the self you are as a 45-year-old woman? Singer points out that we don't really know who we are. That we are not our name, our relationship, our history, our body; that, ultimately, all we are is consciousness—the "me" that's experiencing all the external events and inner emotions. The one aware of thoughts.

❧

Exercise: Think about what you know—and what you don't know—about yourself. Feel the humility that comes from letting go of a false sense of solidity.

---

* Experiences which psychologists suggests are critical to our development.

SUBSECTION C

How We Relate To The Physical Universe And Life In General

WE'VE EXPLORED HOW THINKING LESS OF OURSELVES CAN HELP US RELATE to others and ourselves. Now I'd like to explore humility as it relates to our physical universe and Life in general.

The Path Of Recognizing
Our Rightful Place In The Universe—
Part I: Little "I"S In A Great Big Universe

There's a country song that says "I hope you still feel small when you stand beside the ocean." As we've seen, we are but one small drop in an ocean of consciousness. Another way to put ourselves in perspective is to realize how small we are compared to the Universe. We all know that we are one of billions of people on planet Earth. But did you know that you could fit over one million three hundred thousand planets the size of the Earth inside of the Sun? And that's just for starters. For there's a star called Antares that could fit 64 million stars the size of our Sun inside of it. And then there's a star in the constellation of Hercules that is 100 million times as big as Antares! And—you guessed it—there's another star called Epsilon that could easily swallow up several million stars the size of the one in Hercules! It has been calculated that there are more stars in the universe than there are grains of sand in all of the beaches on the planet. All of this not to mention the vast expanse of space between these stars. This gives me a sense of awe at how vast our universe really is—and how great its Creator.

Exercise: Remind yourself how small you are compared to the rest of the universe.

The Path Of Recognizing
Our Rightful Place In The Universe
Part II: The Path Of Recognizing You Are Not Alone

While it may seem scary to be such a small part of a humongous universe, the Bible tells us that the God who created the vast expanse of space has numbered the very hairs on our head. That is, God knows all about us and everything we're going through. And that somehow all of our trials are working for our good. It is important to note that God has made us the apex of His creation and that we, as humans, can have a relationship with Him that is in some ways more intimate than the other life forms on this Earth.

There's a book out called *When God Winks At You*. It opens with the story of a woman who had been meaning to go to a local church for a long time but had never gone. This same woman was also obsessed with trying to find her birth mother. One day she decided to attend the church, where she happened to sit next to a woman who, coincidentally, told her that she had been looking for her daughter that she hadn't seen since birth. And, you guessed it, it turned out that the two women were mother and daughter!

Although not as impressive as that, I've had many times when I felt God winking at me through coincidences that I, in my sanctified foolishness, take to be a sign from God that He knows all about me and is actively involved in my life. Times when I'll hear a word or a phrase that I haven't heard in years and then hear it again less than an hour later. Or some other remarkable coincidence will occur. People in church call it "confirmation"—a term used to describe divine coincidences, such as when you are reading or thinking about a particular scripture when you wake up and it comes up in the sermon in the afternoon. Or when the preacher preaches on the very thing you are dealing with in your personal life.

One morning when I was wondering how I was going to face the day ahead of me, it dawned on me that I was not alone. That God was engineering my circumstances and that He would be with me and put people in my path that would help me meet my needs and achieve my goals. It was February 3rd, 2018, which was significant in that, when I went to read my daily devotional (Sarah Young's *Jesus Calling*) it started out with the sentence "I am with you and for you. You face nothing alone—*nothing!*"

This is an example of what Jung called "synchronicity." Like the time when I went to my aunt's boyfriend's funeral and was given a sand dollar, only to have one of my clients bring up the spiritual significance of sand dollars the very next day (a striking coincidence as I hadn't thought of or heard anyone mention sand dollars in years!).

Recognizing that we are not alone is a comforting thought and a path to humility. As we recognize our own inability to handle our situations by ourselves, we are reminded that we have God's help and the help of others He has put in our path.

Proverbs 3:5, 6 states "Trust the Lord with all thine heart, and lean not unto thine own understanding. In all thy ways acknowledge Him, and He shall direct thy paths."

If recognizing we can't handle our situations alone isn't enough to humble us and make us look to our Higher Power for help, the path of recognizing how little we truly know about Life itself—and the related path of recognizing how little we control—reminds me, personally to relax my attempts to control my life, and to turn it over to God in faith, knowing that He is in control whether I like it or not.

☙

Exercise: As you go through your day remind yourself that you are but one of billions of people living on a small planet in the middle of outer space. Use this to help you put your problems (I mean "challenges") in perspective.

The Path Of Recognizing How Little We Know (Part I)

One of the paths to humility I find particularly useful is to stop and think about how little I truly *know*. Let me walk you through it. First of all, think about all the things you know you don't know. You don't know the origin of Life. You don't know what's going to happen to you after you die (although you may subscribe to one belief or another). You don't know what's going to happen to you in the next moment.

Now think of the things you think you *do* know. My friend likes to watch Ancient Aliens on the history channel. I get a kick out of this, especially when I see the guy whose hair looks like he just put his finger in a light socket! I laugh as the narrator in his deep, serious voice talks about the beliefs of "ancient alien theorists"—who happen to be the same 5 guys who talk about a range of events that "prove" we've been visited by extra-terrestrials.

But when I stop laughing, it occurs to me that maybe, just maybe, these people are right. Maybe life on Earth DID begin from some alien being.

Maybe they DID build the pyramids. When I humble myself in this way, I can almost accept the possibility that the guys on the ghost shows my friend watches are actually recording paranormal activity on the little Geiger counters they carry around to measure that stuff.

Almost.

Another way of realizing how little we know is to think about the stupid stuff we used to believe. When I was 10, my friends and I would spend our time waiting for a tennis court engaged in scholarly debates over the various properties of Wilson tennis balls. We noted, for example, that Wilson 3s were less bouncy than Wilson 6s, and that the even-numbered balls lasted longer than the odd-numbered ones. The sons of scientists, we approached the topic with all of the brilliance and vigor you would expect of our big-brained fathers, holding a regular Algonquin Table on the subject. Yet it never occurred to us that the numbers MEANT ABSOLUTELY NOTHING AT ALL! Wilson simply put different numbers on their balls so that people on adjacent courts would know whose balls they were.

❧

Exercise: Think back to your childhood and think of the things you used to hold as gospel truth but you now know are patently false. If you didn't have ludicrous discussions about tennis balls, remember what you thought about Santa Claus and the Tooth Fairy. Or where you thought babies came from.

Then remember that much of what you think is true right now will turn out to be false. Let go of false solidity and humble yourself accordingly.

The Path Of Recognizing How Little We Know (Part II)

But it's not just childhood myths that aren't true. We as adults are constantly finding out things we once believed as a society simply aren't true. When I was growing up my mother taught me to eat the yoke of the egg because it was better for me than the white. Now we are told the opposite.

That the yoke will give you cardiac disease. That the white stuff is all good.

I heard about a professor who was teaching a graduate course in quantum physics: "Half of what I'm about to teach you is bullshit," he said, pointing to the fact that our knowledge of physics is still evolving. "The problem is we don't know which half that is!"

In ancient Greece, the Oracle of Delphi named Socrates the wisest man on the planet. His reply? "It must be because I know that I know nothing." Others who were less wise apparently believed that they knew something.

In the 1600s the father of modern philosophy, the Frenchman Rene Descartes, locked himself in a room for twenty years and concluded there were only two things he could know for certain: 1) "I think, therefore I am." And 2) that "God exists because I can prove it." Unfortunately for the rest of us, Descartes' proof of God turned out to be bogus. This led to a philosophical nervous breakdown, with everyone wondering if there was anything we could know. That is, until Immanuel Kant came along a century later and saved the day, pointing out that there had to be certain truths in order for sentient beings to exist. Still, even if we can say for a fact that 2 + 2 must equal 4, there's so much we don't know—including much of what we take for "fact."

When you look back over the centuries, there are many things we took as gospel that aren't true. For the longest time, people thought the Sun revolved around the Earth. Now we think those people were idiots. It is humbling, is it not, to think that a hundred years from now people will think we were idiots for what we believe today? Won't it be something if we get the opportunity after we die to look back over our lives and realize exactly how much we thought we knew and were wrong about?

Yet another way to bring home how little we really know is to meditate on how little we know about cause and effect in our lives. When something happens to us we often think we know what caused it. Yet the more we look into the matter of cause and effect, the more obvious it becomes how little we know.

Was our blessing or misfortune an answer to prayer (and if so, whose prayer—yours or someone else who was praying for you—and was that person someone on this Earth or someone who was praying for you from heaven?)?

Was it something that came about due to the influence of the other planets in our solar system? Or were the stars lined up for or against you (as the astrologists believe)? Was it an act of divine providence. Or was it simply a matter of karma? And if it was karma, was it something done in this life or a past life—or something that wasn't caused by karma at all but something that will be karmically balanced by an event in the future.*

---

* This relates to a revelation I had about karma. That our current situation need not be the result of bad or good karma, either from a past life or this life, but could be an attack of the Enemy which would be rectified by good karma later in life or in the afterlife. While many Christians believe that this afterlife will be in a permanent heaven that we gain access to by accepting Jesus as Lord and Savior, Buddhists believe in "heavenly

Part of the reason we think we know more than we do is that, compared to what people knew in the past, we know quite a lot. Modern science has made great strides in explaining how the universe works. Modern medicine has rapidly evolved from the days when we used leach-therapy, did witch dances to appease the gods, or gave patients lobotomies to control their mental illnesses. Modern technology has in many ways outpaced our ability to control it. Way back in the 1960s, Martin Luther King declared "Our scientific power has outrun our spiritual power. We have guided missiles and misguided men." Imagine what Dr. King would say to us today, with our eyes glued to our smart phones and our nukes more powerful than ever.

The end result of all this is that modern mankind has replaced the superstitions of our ancestors who attributed everything they didn't understand to "the gods," with the myth that we will eventually be able to unlock all of Life's secrets with our minds. What we fail to realize is how much we don't know—and that the more we learn, the more new questions are raised. In this age of rationalism, we believe that everything has a logical explanation. If the first lesson of Copernicus was that the world doesn't revolve around us, the second lesson is that we don't know even the things we think we do.

❦

Exercise: As you go through the day, think about those things we take for granted—and recognize that much of it is going to turn out to be rubbish.

---

realms" and "hellish realms" that are not permanent. This speaks to those who reject the idea of an eternal hell because, as my friend Ed says, "No human being—not even Hitler—could do anything worth suffering for *eternity*. Ten billion years maybe, but eternity—I don't think so." My friend also points out that heaven may not be permanent as, after a good few hundred years or so in heaven, he would be mindful of the Buddhist idea of the Boddhisattva, an enlightened being who vows to return to Earth or another planet where sentient beings were suffering, and, like Jesus, come down from heaven in the name of helping others attain nirvana/enlightenment/salvation.

Death: The Great Unknown

As we discussed in Section I, modern mankind's obsession with rational explanations stems from the desire for control. For if we can understand a thing, we feel as though we can control it. In fact some would say we narrate the world in order to feel we control it. That the little voice in our head is simply a way of trying to command the unfathomable and uncontrollable experience of life itself.

Nothing shows how little we know and control more than the 10,000-pound elephant in the room: Death. As we've seen, we as a society (nay, as a species) have a major problem with death, as it reminds us both of how little we know and how beyond our control our lives really are.

If we don't truly understand life, death is an even greater mystery, as people just don't seem to go and come back again. Even Houdini, who promised he would do his best to escape death, never returned. He didn't even send a text.

Ultimately, death reminds us of the problem of placing ourselves in the center of the universe, where no mortal being—or even race of beings—belongs. It is one of the reasons we are so neurotic. The notion that we are the center or the universe can only make sense if we are eternal. This leads many of us to seek "immortality" through means that cannot possibly provide what can only come from a Spiritual Awakening to our true Immortality (the immortality of the soul and its one-ness with God).

Death And How We Seek To Avoid It

As we discussed, modern mankind finds death so frightening he has devised all manner of ways to avoid it. This includes fame, denial, modern medicine and distractions.

Finally—and quite ironically—we seek to avoid death by arming ourselves to the teeth. This is especially true of us Americans, who, as we've already noted, spend more money on our military than the next 9 nations combined. Back in 2012 when a maniac murdered 26 people including 20 first graders, the National Rifle Association suggested we combat the problem, not by limiting sales of assault rifles like the one used in the massacre, but by ARMING TEACHERS—a call echoed in 2018 by some politicians after an assault rifle-wielding teen killed 17 in a school shooting in Florida. (As a former public school teacher I can picture the scene right now: "Joey, stop pulling Suzie's hair or I'LL BLOW YOUR BRAINS OUT!") After Sandy Hook, the NRA promoted a gun for young children called "The Cricket." Shortly thereafter a 5-year-old killed his 2-year-old sister with one. Who could've foreseen *that* happening?

Of course, our desire to thwart death for as long as possible serves several useful purposes, as it promotes survival of the individual and the species. Thus we are "hard-wired" to do everything we can to avoid our passing on to another state, no matter how inevitable that may be.

The Path Of Developing
A Healthy Relationship With Death

Death can be very frightening if a person doesn't have a sense of their own spirituality or a faith in something larger than themselves. I myself came close to a nervous breakdown as a college freshman when I had an existential crisis, as the prospect of my own mortality led me to ponder the meaninglessness of my own existence.

Fortunately, God stepped in and gave me the epiphany that I was a Spiritual Being in a physical body that would continue to exist long after Daniel Cohen died. God also graciously revealed to me that He* did, indeed, exist, and that on some deep level He and I were One (or at least my soul was part of the divine Soul).

But you don't need to have a religious experience to recognize that death is a vitally important part of life to be appreciated rather than feared.

One way to appreciate the value of death is to imagine what life would be like without death. While that might sound appealing at first, think of the drawbacks. In addition to inevitable overpopulation, there would be no work for morticians, Halloween would be ruined, and if you got married, it would no longer be "Till death do us part"— a horrifying thought to those who've taken the vows!

All joking aside, what would eternal life look like for someone who is being tortured? In the TV series *Game of Thrones*, a nun who had been persecuting the evil queen Cercei Lannister finds the tables turned and in the queen's dungeon. When the woman, after being taunted by Cercei, declares that she is ready to die, Cercei replies:

"So soon? Oh no. You are going to be dying for a long, long time!"

---

* I use the male pronoun for simplicity's sake but recognize God has no gender.

Death limits the amount of suffering one human being can endure. Death also makes life precious by giving us a time limit—imagine how much those of us who like to procrastinate would do with unlimited time!

⁂

Exercise: Stop and think about all the problems that could arise if there were no death. Then be grateful for its existence.

Five Lessons Death Has To Teach Us

We've already seen how death teaches us how little we know. For the remainder of this section we'll explore five other lessons death has to teach us and the paths to humility that stem from them.

THE LESSON OF CONTEMPLATING DEATH #1:
Treat Every Moment As Precious

THE FIRST AND MOST OBVIOUS LESSON DEATH HAS TO TEACH US IS THAT every moment is precious. We all have the choice to focus on the parts of our lives that are half-full or half-empty. More than our circumstances themselves, it's this choice that determines our level of happiness. Contemplating the fact that we could die at any moment leads to two paths to humility. First, that we DON'T waste our precious time focusing on negative thoughts, and, second, that we DO live each day to the fullest, knowing it could be our last—two excellent paths to combat depression and boredom.

The Path Of Not Wasting What Could Be Your Last Thought On Planet Earth On Something Negative

When you find yourself stewing about something someone said or did to you earlier in the day, it's a good time to ask yourself if you want to waste what potentially could be your last thought on Earth on this. In fact, it's a good question to ask yourself whenever you are getting upset over something that happened in the past or worrying about something you are going to face in the future.

Simply put, we remind ourselves that the negative thought you are having about your boss, your spouse, your teenager—or the jerk that just cut you off in traffic—could be your last. Do you really want to waste your last thought on something so negative and trivial? Wouldn't you rather be thinking about someone you love or some beautiful experience you've had?

One problem I struggle with is a propensity to worry about difficult situations I'm facing. What helps is recognizing I don't want this worry thought to be my last. Essentially my thought process goes like this: "Do I really want *this* to be my last thought on planet Earth—especially when the situation I'm worried about may never take place, as something may change—including the possibility that I won't be on this planet when this event is supposed to occur?" This could apply to worrying about a business meeting, a looming confrontation with your spouse or teenager, or starting a new job.

☙

Exercise: View the negative thoughts that go through your mind through the prism of your mortality, challenging yourself not to waste your time on them.

The Path Of Living Like
This Could Be Your Last Day On Planet Earth

I f one of death's lessons is not to focus on the negative, another is to focus on the positive and appreciate the Heck out of it. For while it's fairly easy to see how humility leads to serenity, humility can also make life more thrilling as well. Think about how much vitality it would add to your life if you saw each encounter with another human being as potentially the last one you would ever have. It's said that people who know they are dying live life more intensely and passionately than others. They don't have time for petty jealousies and hatreds. For arguing with their spouses and loved ones. They become truly focused on enjoying the last remaining moments they have on this earth. Living each day as if it may be your last is an excellent way to develop a humble attitude.

In high school I suffered from a chronic ruptured appendix that took two 3-hour operations, 8 inches of my colon and nearly cost me my life. I believe this near-death experience was one of the greatest blessings God gave me, as it made me realize both how precious my time on Earth was and how little control I had. This leads to the next great lesson of death. That we are not in control.

∞

Exercise: Live today as if it could be your last day on earth, savoring every interaction as the special gift it is.

THE LESSON OF CONTEMPLATING DEATH #2:

Letting Go Of Control

As I mentioned in the first section of the book, modern man is a control freak. One of the great lessons death has to teach us is that we are not even in control of when our very existence will end. This brings to mind the great book The Wisdom of Insecurity by Alan Watts, who encourages us to stop worrying about the future and live in the present moment. For while we can't control our circumstances we can control our mind's reaction to said circumstances. Once we realize this, we come to see that trying to control others only gives them more control over ourselves. We can also learn to trust Life and our higher power and finally, to recognize that we do have some control, albeit limited, over what happens to us in this life.

The Path Of Recognizing We Are Not In Control

Death reminds us that our very existence can be snatched away from us in an instant no matter how we try to avoid it. It doesn't matter how wealthy we are, how careful we are, or how advanced our medical team. If it's our time to go, death will have the final say no matter how we strive to keep it at bay.

This is frightening to modern men and women, since we as a species have done much to control our environment and eliminate all natural predators.

Once we recognize how little we control, the next step is to decide what to do about it. Essentially we have two choices: 1) Be scared to death and do everything we can to stave off the inevitable, or 2) Relax, knowing that, since we can't control when we'll leave the planet, the only logical decision is to enjoy our limited time on earth, letting go of our desire to control what we cannot.

The Roller Coaster Analogy

In some ways life is like a roller coaster ride. It has a beginning and an end, and once you get on you have no control over how long the ride will last.* In between you can either enjoy the ups and downs or dread them. Life is either a ride you wish would never end, or something you wish would be over as soon as possible.

Roller coaster riders have two options. Hold on tight and try to control the ride. Or relax and enjoy it. Which option you choose is up to you. Life is either thrilling or a threat to your existence. Life becomes scary when we try to control it, as our inability to avoid death is something which, logically, should scare the living bejeezus out of us.

---

* Excluding suicide which, as we'll explore later, is almost never a good option.

There are, after all, countless ways in which we can die and no way to guarantee it won't happen to us at any time.

This kind of logic will drive you crazy. However a deeper logic—that, given our inability to control death we might as well not worry about it—leads to the Path of Faith.

ℰᴐ

Exercise: Think about how little control we truly have over how long we will be on this earth. Then, instead of giving into fear, embrace it, reminding yourself that trying to control what cannot be controlled is counterproductive.

The Path Of Having Faith
That Everything Will Be Alright

Ultimately if you want to enjoy your life you have to put aside fear and have faith that everything will be alright. This faith may or may not be religious. You can, for instance, remind yourself that the universe has supported you for the past x number of years. That you've survived many trials in the past. That many of the things you feared would destroy you either never came to pass or were much less serious than you thought they'd be.

That said, having a relationship with my Creator has certainly helped me fear death—and life's trials—less. All five major religions believe in the soul's existence after death. So while death may have the final say over our earthly lives, it has no power to end our Existence. What's more, those of us who have a relationship with our Higher Power recognize that He has control over death and will not let death take us before we have fulfilled His purposes for us here on Earth.

In church they say "let go and let God." That is, let go of your problems and turn them over to God and let Him handle them. A deacon in the church I once belonged to used to laugh at people who came to the altar to give their problems over to God, and then showed by their worried faces that they'd picked them back up before they got back to their seats. This illustrates the difference between what we can and can't control. For while the parishioners could control whether they gave their problems up or not, their problems were still there to be picked up again if they so chose.

Exercise: Remind yourself that you've been taken care of by God/the Universe for all of your life thus far. Now trust these cosmic forces to keep you in the future as well. Have faith that death is not necessarily the end of your Existence.

The Path Of Recognizing
What We Can And Cannot Control:
The First Paradox Of Control

This brings us to the first paradox of control. That most of us try to control what we cannot and spend very little effort trying to control what we can.

Essentially, what we *can* control is what goes on inside of our minds and what we *can't* control is everything outside of us. Developing humility is all about controlling our thought/emotional life and letting go of our attempts to control everything else, including our spouses, our teenagers, and our mothers-in-law.

Now this gets a bit complicated. For some would argue—and I would agree—that our minds are often filled with all kinds of disturbing thoughts and emotions, and that, furthermore, any attempt to "control" the mind will only backfire as we will either lose the battle now or merely suppress the thoughts and emotions which will come back to bite us in the future.

So it's not that we *control* the mind, but we control how much we listen to it. We can learn not to react—not only to the stuff the external world throws at us, but to the ridiculous and neurotic things the mind tries to tell us.

Furthermore, we can train our minds to be at peace even when we are having disturbed thoughts and emotions. That said, the goal of this book is retraining out minds so that we have fewer negative thoughts and emotions; to think thoughts that make us feel humbly grateful for being a part of the great big canvass of Life instead of feeling upset because life isn't going exactly according to our wishes.

The Dalai Lama says that a well-trained mind will be able to withstand even the most devastating events with calm and tranquility, while an undisciplined mind can be disturbed by the slightest inconvenience. This brings up the difference between Western and Eastern values.

Exercise: Remember that a trained mind can withstand severe circumstances while an untrained mind is bothered by the slightest disturbance. Vow to train your mind and start meditating, developing a prayer ritual or reading books like the ones recommended in this book that help you train your mind (this could include reading and re-reading the paths in this book so they become second nature).

My Experience Of East And West

B ack when I was in college I was thinking of becoming a philosophy major. After a while I came to the conclusion that, in Western philosophy, the biggest brain won. That the smarter philosopher would convince us that he or she was right, while lesser philosophers, *even if they were right*, would lose the day.

I didn't like that. In particular because my brain is not as smart as many others. I also didn't like the fact that Western philosophers were evaluated solely on their philosophy regardless of how they lived.

Then I had a religious experience while reading Hindu and Buddhist texts that were designed to "enlighten" the reader by helping him or her have a spiritual experience. This piqued my interest in Eastern philosophy which focused on a) having spiritual experiences and b) living in harmony as part of the larger whole that is the universe. Here I was pleased to find that Eastern philosophers were judged on how they lived their lives as well as their philosophy. The goal was to help others have spiritual experiences and live in harmony, not to prove that they were smarter than everyone else.

Not surprisingly, Western philosophers didn't consider Eastern philosophy to be on a par with them, and banished Eastern philosophy to the religion department. And so I became a religion major, where I countered the West's conceit with a conceit of my own: I viewed all Western religions—Judaism, Christianity and Islam—as merely "religions of the word" that did not have the deep spirituality found in Eastern religion but only told you how to live your life—and so were essentially worthless to a rebellious college student who wasn't interested in following anyone's rules.

This, of course, is not only a sweeping generalization, it is patently false, as I would discover one day in 1993 when I first encountered the Holy Spirit as a "tingling sensation" in a predominantly Caucasian church. And then again, in 1996, when I "caught the Holy Ghost" in an African American church—experiences so powerful I went from being a Buddhist to a Christian.

While Western churches do indeed focus on changing our inner attitudes towards life, helping us relate better to God and our fellow humans, Western *society* as a whole tends to be more concerned with the external, focusing on appearances and how to manipulate the world to get what we want. We in the West tend to believe that material success is what makes us happier, so that we seek more-to-be-happy-with instead of trying to be happier with what we already have. As we've seen, *It's Not all About You!* has Eastern tendencies, as the goal of this book is to change the way you look at life, helping you be less insecure and more content with what you already have. However, I would be a hypocrite if I denied that I liked cool new stuff too. There is nothing inherently wrong with enjoying our smart phones or appreciating a good show on our flat screen TVs, and it is worth noting that Eastern societies are following our lead in this respect, and are clamoring for more new "stuff" too. Something we talked about earlier in our discussion of "Consumerism." Furthermore, as we'll soon see, it isn't so simple that West is wrong and East is right. For we do have some, albeit limited, control over how we live our lives even if we can't control the moment of our death.

The Path Of Controlling What Can Be Controlled
(The Benefits Of A Disciplined Mind)

"The true practice of the Dharma is internal;
it is a peaceful, open, and generous mind,
a mind that we know how to train,
that is completely in our control."

— The Dalai Lama, *Essential Teachings*

We humans have been blessed with a tremendous ability to think. We can use our big brains to think of all the ways we could die and to contemplate everything we don't like about life. Or we can use our big brains to think of everything we like about life. We can also contemplate—and have a relationship with—The Being who created us and the universe in which we live, giving thanks for all the beauty we find on the journey.

I used to worry a lot. And while I still worry more than I'd like, humility keeps my worry in check. First, by recognizing that, as the title of this book suggests, it is "not all about me." That I am just a piece of a much larger puzzle. (An important piece, just like you, but a piece nonetheless.) Second, by helping me accept all that I don't like about life (including the inevitability and unpredictability of death) and third, by helping me to be grateful for what I do like.

My favorite statement about humility came from a preacher who said "You can be humbly grateful or grumbly hateful." That, while we can't always control our circumstances, we can <u>choose</u> to either be humbly grateful for what we *do* have or dissatisfied with what we *don't* have. There are people walking around with next to nothing in their pockets who are perfectly content, and there are millionaires who are unhappy because they're not billionaires.

Happiness, it turns out, is a *choice*—one that is completely within our control. And choosing to be happy and choosing to be humble are one in the same.

❦

Exercise: Consider The Serenity Prayer of A.A. substituting "humility" for "serenity."

> Lord, give me the <u>humility</u> to
> accept the things I cannot change
> The courage to change the things I can
> And the wisdom to know the difference

The Path Of Being Less Controlled
By Others And External Events
By Relinquishing Our Desire To Control Them

While we can't entirely control our thoughts and emotions, we *can* control how much they control us. This leads to the second paradox of control: That the more we give up our desire to control others and the world around us, the less control other people and external events have over us.

We try to control our wives, our husbands, our children, our bosses. Even our worry, when properly analyzed, is a misguided attempt to control our circumstances.

Letting go of our desire to control others helps us accept their bad behavior without getting stressed about it and gives us the freedom of not having our happiness controlled by their actions. Letting go of our desire to control events in a universe that is constantly changing in ways we can't control helps us be less bothered when things don't go our way.

The best thing to do when someone is getting on your last nerve is to wish them well or, if you are religiously inclined, to pray for them. Not a short, un-heartfelt prayer, but a sincere, deeply felt prayer for their benefit. When you can get to that point where you really want them to have the desires of their heart (provided those desires are for their betterment), you will feel a deep inner peace and that person will no longer be controlling you as they would be if you were harboring resentment.

When you wish the best for someone who is tormenting you, you let go of your resentment and stop carrying them around with you. This reminds me of the following story. "Two monks are walking by a river when they spot a woman trying to cross. She is too short to cross safely, so one of the monks offers to carry her over on his shoulders. The monk does this, then returns and the two monks continue on their way. A mile later the other monk, infuriated, asks why the first monk defiled himself with the woman. 'Oh, that woman," the first monk replies, "I stopped carrying her a mile ago.'"

Taking this one step further, we can try not to let any of life's events disturb our happiness. This is indeed difficult. In actuality, the goal is to become *less* stressed by life's ups and downs by not holding on to negative events (to stop replaying them over and over in your mind), or worrying about something that is going to happen in the future. As Michael Singer put it so succinctly in one of his talks, "If you're bothered by the future, you're creating a future that doesn't exist that bothers you."

Exercise: Stop trying to control what cannot be controlled. This includes not being disturbed by past events and not projecting negative experiences in the future. Remind yourself that the less you try to control what you cannot, the less control events and other people have over you.

The Path Of Not Worrying
About The Wellbeing Of Others:
A Personal Confession

A friend of mine told me that he often worried about others. Not what they thought of him, but that he was concerned for their well-being. Did my book have anything to say about that?

My first thought was what an absolute jerk I was that I almost never worried about anyone but myself and my immediate family. That, in fact, I once sat in a Bible study next to my wife's godfather who was talking about how grateful he was that he'd gotten good news about a potentially life-threatening blood clot, and all I could think was that it really didn't matter whether he lived much longer or not since he had no great work to do like the one God had given me with my humility book. Yes, that thought not only crossed my mind, I actually *entertained* it. It is one of my most sinful thoughts and I am deeply ashamed of it.

This is what the Christian writer Oswald Chambers means when he says that, when we bother to look at ourselves closely, we realize that we are the greatest sinners who ever lived. I mean, this thought, so vile, so heinous, from a pastor in the Church of Jesus Christ, a man writing a book on humility no less; that this thought could come to me, how much of a leap is that to Adolph Hitler contemplating the extermination of 6 million Jews?

Next I thought that humility was not concerned with my friend's issue.

That someone who worried about what was happening to others was displaying humility, not in need of it.

Finally, I came to my senses and realized that humility indeed had quite a bit to say about my friend's predicament. That while his compassion was to be lauded, his worry was, in fact, something that could be helped by a hefty dose of humility, which could remind him not to worry about things we can't control, including other peoples' health and whatever situations they face that we don't have the power to help them with. Things we have to leave up to our Higher Power.

Exercise: Remember that you are not responsible for other people's welfare and give up worrying about situations involving loved ones that you cannot help them with. This does not mean abandoning your responsibilities, it just means recognizing your limitations.

The Path Of Recognizing
Our Inability To Control Our Lives
And Turning Them Over To A Higher Power

Alcoholics Anonymous speaks to the addict's inability to control his or her desire to drink and the need to turn one's life over to a power greater than oneself. We who are self-aholics (and I believe that covers most of us alive today), have the same option to turn our lives over to a Power greater than ourselves.

Are you willing to give up your right to yourself? Paradoxically, our willingness to give up our right to what we think will make us happy actually makes us happy in the end. Giving up our right to ourselves by letting God have His way in our lives, to whatever extent we are able to do it, is the key to a humility that gives us lasting peace.

It means giving up our "bad pride" (there is "good pride" which we'll explore in the next section), our need to outdo others, the excitement we get from running around feeling self-important, our need to leave our mark on this world. In short, giving up our addiction to self. This is no easy task, as the addiction to self may well be the strongest addiction of all.

Humility also takes courage as it asks us to give up our need to protect ourselves. To accept Life on Her terms. To see ourselves as part of Nature rather than fighting it. From this perspective death is not a threat, but part of the life cycle.

But being free from the fear of death is only one of the benefits of humility. As we break the bondage of self-obsession, we experience Life in all of its fullness. As singer/guitarist/philosopher Jimi Hendrix put it "I used to live in a room full of mirrors, all I could see was me. Now I take my Spirit and I smash my mirrors. Now the whole world is there for me to see!"

With God at the center of our lives, we revolve around our eternal Creator the way the Earth revolves around the Sun. For while having the world revolve around us was tempting, we've seen how that leads to a life out of harmony with Nature. As for the wonders of modern technology, I am not suggesting we discard them. For there is nothing inherently wrong with enjoying the fruits of modern technology AS LONG AS WE PUT GOD FIRST. Or, as Alcoholics Anonymous states, *as long as we put humility first.*

Putting God in the center of our universe restores balance and harmony, curing the anxiety and depression caused by putting a finite being in the center of the universe. This does not diminish us, it puts us in our rightful place. The Earth has a wonderful place in the solar system just as humanity has a wonderful place in creation. The Sun gives light and life to Earth. It cherishes her. Just so, God cherishes us, his crowning achievement.

For mankind is God's most advanced creation to date, and God has given us dominion over the Earth and helped us unlock Her secrets. The animals worship God unconsciously. If humans are the only earthlings foolish enough to try to take God's place, we alone are capable of willful worship. This gives us a special relationship with our Creator. For ultimately Consumerism must be replaced by some form of God-ism, whether in the form of the God of organized religion or A.A.'s "higher power."

This brings up the question, "Do you need to believe in God in order to be humble?" Let me answer that with the punchline to a joke about a Jewish mother who comes to the aid of a man who just broke his leg skiing by bringing him a bowl of chicken soup. "Lady, I just broke my leg! What good will that chicken soup do me?" To which the Jewish mother replies, "Well, it couldn't hurt!"

But seriously there are several ways to answer this question. Some say it is impossible to be humble without recognizing one's dependence on God. And if you take seriously the notion that we are all addicted to "self" to some degree, you could apply Alcoholics Anonymous' viewpoint that we must "Make a decision to turn our will and our lives over to the care of God *as we understand Him*." That said, I have a friend I consider to be humble who does not believe in a creator God (and neither do most Buddhists, including the Dalai Lama)—but for me my relationship with God has been central to my walk with humility.

If God-talk makes you uncomfortable, I apologize, but would humbly ask you to ask yourself *why* it bothers you. Could it be that you are too proud to accept that there is a God who holds your very existence in His hands?

Accepting a Higher Power is a cornerstone to A.A., with five of the twelve steps mentioning the word "God" by name, and I believe it is a key component to humility. A.A. founder Bill Wilson agrees. On page 75 of *Twelve steps and Twelve Traditions* he writes:

> **"During this process of learning more about humility, the most profound result of all was the change in our attitude toward God**...The notion that we would still live our own lives, God helping a little now and then, began to evaporate...now the words "Of myself I am nothing, the Father doeth the works" began to carry bright promise and meaning. We saw we needn't always be bludgeoned and beaten into humility. It could come quite as much from our voluntary reaching for it as it could from unremitting suffering."

Turning our lives over to God means letting go of our desire to control our roller coaster ride and relaxing and going with the flow of where God is taking us. This is made easier by developing faith and having a relationship with the Almighty. As we get to know our Creator better, we come to know the path He wants us to be on.

Jesus says that all of God's commandments boil down to loving God and loving our fellow human beings. This gives us a general idea of what God wants us to do, but it's not very specific.

Why doesn't God just tell us precisely what He wants each of us to do on this Earth? One reason may be that He gave us free will and doesn't want to coerce us into obeying His commandments. Another is that He wants us to figure it out on our own. While He does give us hints along the way, ultimately the reason He doesn't tell most of us (myself included) what He wants us to do *directly* is something we simply don't know—yet another reason to subscribe to the Path of Recognizing How Little We Know.

Exercise: Recognize your limitations as a finite mortal and turn your life over to your Higher Power.

The Path Of Taking Responsibility For
The Limited Control We Have Over Our Lives

While we can't keep death at bay if it's our time to go, we do have some limited control over how long we stay on the planet and the lives we lead while we are here. It has been said that we should pray as if everything depended on God, and act as if everything depends upon us. And while we've seen that we can't really "control" in an absolute sense anything that happens outside of our minds, this does not mean we have *no* control over what happens to us.

This is one way life is definitely NOT like a roller coaster. For when you are on a roller coaster you have no control whatsoever over the ups and downs. You simply have the ability to let go or hang on tight in a desperate attempt to control what you cannot.

Unlike being on a roller coaster, life does allow us some limited control over what happens to us. At one extreme there are those of us who decide to commit suicide. And while I encourage anyone who's considering this option to recognize that it is a permanent solution to a temporary problem—one that will cause heartache to those left behind—there are many things people do short of killing themselves that limit their life span. This includes being overweight, taking unnecessary risks, not taking care of our health and not following our doctor's advice.

I'm reminded of the story of the Rabbi who wants to win the lottery. He prays to God "Lord, let me win the lottery."

He doesn't win.

So he pleads with God. "God, I've been a good Rabbi. I've kept your commandments and led your people in the ways of the Torah. Lord, please let me win the lottery."

Again, he doesn't win.

Finally, he begs God to help him win the lottery. "God, I don't understand why you've failed me so far! You know how much I need the money. My kids are going off to college and I can't afford the tuition. Lord I beg of you please, *please* let me win the lottery!

Suddenly a voice comes booming down from heaven. "Moshe," He says. "Meet me halfway—buy a ticket!"

Exercise: Recognize that you have limited control over your life and use your will to benefit yourself and others to whatever extent possible.

THE LESSON OF CONTEMPLATING DEATH #3

You Can't Take It With You: Three Path Of Stewardship

WEBSTER DEFINES STEWARDSHIP AS "THE CAREFUL AND RESPONSIBLE management of something entrusted to one's care." Death teaches us that that "something" is our lives and everything in them, including our relationships and all that we own.

Death puts an "ownership obsessed" society in its place, reminding us that we are but stewards of all we "own" on this Earth, as we can't take any of it with us when we die. This is a very hard concept to grasp in a society so obsessed with material possessions. A society that is constantly trying to market new products. A society where you're judged by the house you live in or the car you drive.

Death teaches us that everything we have is leased to us and returned to others the day we die. In so doing, it embraces the Native American idea of "ownership" over the European idea we see in modern day America.

So what are we to do? Humility suggests…

The Path Of Appreciating What You Have More Rather Than Looking For More To Appreciate

This path challenges you to *appreciate what you have more* rather than seeking more to appreciate. While it is extremely beneficial to all who practice it, this path is not popular in the West because it runs counter to its basic assumptions of what makes you happy.

We live in a society where the goal of life is to become happier by getting more things to appreciate—a society where the motto seems to be "He who dies with the most toys wins." As mentioned earlier, humility suggests we seek to appreciate what we already have more. This doesn't mean we have to stop obtaining new things and experiences. On the contrary, the more humble we become the more God and others will want to bless us with whatever we desire.

This path is better than Consumerism's path of seeking to get more to appreciate for two reasons. First, to appreciate what you have more, you don't have to get something you don't already have. This means you do not have to worry about the possibility you may never attain it. Second, it promotes happiness NOW. If you stop to think about it, looking for happiness in the future doesn't make much sense. Take for example the stressed out businessman who works hard so he can take a vacation and then can't enjoy himself because he doesn't know how to relax. Furthermore, if you're not happy now, what makes you think you'll be happier with that new toy, that new promotion? Most people find that the new thing only makes them happy for a short time. Then they're off looking for the next thing.

Ultimately true peace doesn't come from getting new things, but from taking a humbly grateful attitude towards those things we DO possess.

Advertisers are screaming at you "You need this!" and "You need that!" Stand back and say, "No, I don't need this, and I don't need that" and feel the peace that comes with it. Shoot, there's a whole religion devoted to letting go of stuff called Buddhism. Simply put, several hundred years before Christ walked the Earth, the Buddha discovered that being attached to things was the root cause of all pain, and that the chain of unhappiness could only be broken through letting go of all attachments. And, sure enough, once the mind was liberated, the Buddha was able to attain enlightenment—a transcendent state that is not unlike catching the Holy Ghost although much quieter and more meditative.

Exercise: Go through your day focusing on appreciating what you have more.

The Path Of Thinking About How Much Good Karma We Can Create In The Day (In The Hopes Of A Blessing In This Life Or The Afterlife)

S tewardship means that not only do we benefit from what we've been given in this life, we are *responsible* for all we are stewards over. More than just appreciating what we have more, we are to take care of what we have and use our time, money and talents to bless our brothers and sisters for not only is this the right thing to do, it will benefit us in the long run.

If we are here today and gone tomorrow, that doesn't mean we are gone for good. Eastern religions all assume two principals: The law of karma (that is, that everything you do comes back to you) and reincarnation. These two principals go hand in hand, as the idea is that we live in a just universe where everyone will get their reward for what they do, and any good or bad karma that they aren't rewarded for on Earth will be taken care of in their next life.

These two laws are reflected in Western religions as well. In the book of Galatians the Bible says that we will "reap what we sow." Many Jews, Christians and Muslims believe they will get rewarded for their deeds (karma) by getting into heaven or hell (a reincarnation of sorts) as the result of their deeds on Earth.

The notion of karma gets tricky in Christianity, as we are granted heaven because of our acceptance of Jesus as Lord and Savior, not because we've done good deeds. Yet while we don't get into heaven because we do good works, we do good works nonetheless because we are trying to follow Jesus' example and live by Biblical commandments, all of which, Jesus taught, come down to just two: Love God and love your fellow humans.

Furthermore, we have internal reasons to do good, as the Holy Spirit inside of us reacts negatively when we do bad things, convicting us of sin. This is not to suggest that all who profess to be Christians are good people (as we recognize that all have sinned and fallen short of the glory of God)—just that those who are "true Christians," like true believers in all faiths, are doing our best to live lives pleasing to God.

৶

Exercise: Think of ways to create good karma for yourself today, reminding yourself it will benefit you in the long run.

The Path Of Doing Good For Goodness Sake

While there's nothing wrong with doing good out of one's own self-interest, the noblest path of a good steward is to do good for the sake of doing good. Or, for those of us who believe in Him, for doing good to please Our Maker whether He rewards us for it or not. The Dalai Lama, who doesn't believe in a Creator God, calls this "enlightened self-interest," pointing to the interconnectedness of our beings. This is also bolstered by the notion that we are all "other me's" (something we discussed back in path #2), so that by helping others, you are actually helping "yourself" by helping another with the same human consciousness.

Ironically, doing good for goodness' sake—instead of for the good karma you will get out of it—actually creates MORE good karma than you'd get from doing good for karma's sake! After all, when it comes to our actions, our motives are critical to determining if we've done "good" or "bad."

☙

Exercise: Do something good for someone else today without expecting anything in return.

THE LESSON OF CONTEMPLATING DEATH #4:

The Path Of Not Being In A Hurry— And The Related Path Of Listening

SINCE WE CAN'T OUTRUN DEATH, WE NEED TO RELAX AND GO WITH THE flow of life. Much of our anxiety comes from getting out of sync with the rhythm of life. Like a basketball player out of the flow of the game, we lose our spiritual center. People who are in a hurry are particularly self-centered, focusing on what they need to accomplish and failing to take the time to appreciate life and to listen to the people they encounter. Death reminds us that this "all about me" attitude is pointless, reminding us that as we are all going to die one day, we might as well relax and enjoy those moments we have on planet Earth.

The Path Of Not Being In A Hurry

I'm in a hurry to get things done
I rush and rush until life's no fun
All I really gotta do is live and die
But I'm in a hurry and don't know why

— "I'm in a Hurry" by country group Alabama

In 1982 Godfrey Reggio directed the movie "Koyaanisqatsi" (coy-yan-as-katsi)—a Hopi Indian term for "life out of balance." In the movie he showed how modern life has gotten out of control, with humans living at a frenetic pace that is markedly different from life in nature.

Modern technology has increased the pace at which we live in ways our ancestors couldn't have dreamed of. With less energy than it takes to say "Let there be light!" we flick a switch and make it so. Turn the faucet and the river comes to us. Click the remote and we access a world of entertainment.

Airplanes allow us to get where we're going ten times faster than taking a car (which, in itself, is a heck of a lot faster than walking, running or riding on horseback). And that's just the beginning. Today we send messages and talk to and see other human beings all over the globe, all with hand-held devices that take pictures, play games and access the internet, providing us with instant answers to critical questions like "Who was Monica Lewinsky and what did she do to Bill Clinton?" Of course, cell phones are evolving faster than ever, so it is not enough to do all that. Consumerism's First Commandment demands that you must have the latest model: "Thou shalt not let the Joneses pass you by!"

So while we *could* wait until our old cell phones die to replace them, we won't, not only because we'd be out of fashion, but because if there's one thing we gods and goddesses don't do, it's wait. The watchword today is "NOW." Not the Zen Buddhist's eternal "Now" of the present moment, but the infantile "I want it NOW!" of a spoiled 3-year-old. Carl Jung, the founder of analytic psychology, once wrote "Hurry is not of the devil, it IS the devil." We moderns are firmly in the devil's grip, running the rat race in order to get the newest stuff lest we buy something that is out of fashion.

One of the lessons of death is that, try as we may, we simply cannot outrun it. Our problem is, the more we hurry, the less we live in the moment. When you are in a hurry, you not only miss out on fully experiencing the present moment, you tend to be anything but humble and wind up upsetting those around you as you hurry past them without interacting with them on a deeper level. People who are in a rush tend to be extremely self-centered and have little or no time to listen to the concerns of those around them. This can affect your relationships at home, at work, and in the community—as I found out the other day when I had a humiliating experience in the express lane at a Price Rite grocery store.

As is often the case when I go to the supermarket, I was in a hurry, so I counted my items to make sure I could go in the "15 items or less" lane to purchase my groceries. I was right at the limit, and right behind me were two people who had only one or two items each. But instead of doing the right thing and letting them go ahead of me, I pretended not to notice them because I was hungry, having just gotten out of church, and was in a hurry to eat some of the groceries I was buying. The fact that I was a Caucasian male dressed in a suit did not help my cause.

Anyway, as the Hispanic cashier finished with the person in front of me, she turned to me and, in a not too pleasant voice, informed me that this was an express lane and that I was over the limit—but that she would let me through as I had already put my groceries on the conveyer belt.

Now I had been a bagger for Stop and Shop some years ago, and was taught that if a customer had a number of items that were the same, they counted as one item.

When I protested that I had counted and only had 15 items, the cashier pointed to the 8 cans of tuna which put me well over the limit. I explained that I thought they counted as one, and the young African American male supervisor who happened to be at the register confirmed that the store policy was that each one of my cans of tuna fish counted as a separate item.

This was very embarrassing.

℣

Folks like to say they are tired of waiting patiently. This is a lie. When you are patient, you are at peace. In fact, just as we replaced the word "serenity" with "humility" in the serenity prayer, we could easily replace it with "patience" as well.

"Lord give me the *patience* to accept the things I cannot change…"

What people really mean when they say they are tired of waiting patiently is that they are tired of waiting IM-patiently. We as a society are all about instant gratification. We're spoiling ourselves and I'm afraid it's only going to get worse for the next generation. When I was growing up, we had cartoons on Saturday mornings and a couple hours after school. Now it's 24/7. When I was young if we wanted to look at dirty pictures we had to wait until we got up the courage to buy a magazine at the local drug store and risk getting laughed at by the old man behind the counter. Today there's pornography our children can access on the internet any time they want.

Having things come to us faster and faster seems like a blessing, but it is not. For our need for speed quickly turns to annoyance the moment we are forced to wait for something. In so doing we are failing to form the disciplined mind the Dalai Lama talks about in the quotation in path #31.

So many of our "problems" can be solved by a little patience. Patience allows us to do things in God's time and not demand that they be done instantaneously. Patience is like a muscle that needs to be exercised, but we moderns are doing everything we can to avoid using it. Trying to make things happen more and more quickly leads to frustration.

I remember the first time I discovered that my phone would help me write my text messages. At first, I was delighted to see that, when I typed in a few letters, I would immediately have the option to press on the entire word which the phone had figured out before I finished typing it! Yet I quickly became used to the convenience and then, instead of being grateful for it, I not only took it for granted, I started getting annoyed when the phone didn't anticipate the word I was typing fast enough!

No wonder there's so much road rage. When you're stuck in a traffic jam, are you thinking about how grateful you are that you're driving an automobile when a hundred years ago you'd have to be walking? Or are you getting upset that the car isn't taking you where you're going as fast as you're used to?

This problem is more pronounced in Americans and is most pronounced in urban centers where life moves faster than the rural areas. In downtown New York City it's not uncommon to see people running on the street trying to get to their next appointment. The fast-paced life is a temptation. When you're in a hurry you are only thinking of yourself and the "mission" you have to accomplish.

Some of us are familiar with the Bobby McFerrin song "Don't Worry, Be Happy." But I'd like to make the case for "Don't hurry, be happy." Hurry is a MAJOR humility issue in that when we hurry we are obsessing about what WE have to accomplish. We are so focused on what we have to do that we don't have time to stop and help someone else. And while we may not be the only generation to struggle with hurry, it is a symptom of modern mankind, one reflected in the rapid expansion of Dunkin Donuts and Starbucks.

Humility requires us to slow down and appreciate the moment we are currently living in rather than being in a hurry to get to the next event. There's a sect of Buddhism called Zen Buddhism that specifically talks about the importance of staying in the moment, focusing on doing one thing at a time.

How different is that from the way we go about our days, trying to eat breakfast while we're driving to work, thinking about what we're going to do when we get there rather than focusing on the road. It's this constant thinking ahead that keeps us from being at peace.

When you're in a hurry, you are like a basketball player out of the flow of the game. As I like to remind folks there's no place in the Bible where it says, "And Jesus did no miracles there because he was in a hurry to get home for supper." Once you start to slow down, you can treat each moment as the precious gift it is.

Now I'm not saying we always have to take it slow. We have to have a sense of balance. To know when it's appropriate to move quickly. Folk singer Cat Stevens (now a devout Muslim known as Yusuf Islam) has a great line in his song On The Road to Find Out: "I listen to the wind come howl, telling me I have to hurry. I listen to the Robbin's song saying not to worry."

If you are always present and experiencing each moment fully, you will find time to help others when the occasion arises. This also involves the art of listening.

ℰℐ

Exercise: Let someone ahead of you in a grocery line. Relax and meditate or enjoy the music on your radio when stuck in a traffic jam. Pray for the driver who cuts you off in traffic.

The Path Of Listening

The amplified version of the book of James, chapter 1 verse 19 reads as follows: "Be quick to hear [be a careful, thoughtful listener], slow to speak [a speaker of carefully chosen words and], slow to anger [patient, reflective, forgiving]..."

We think great conversationalists are people who talk a lot, but what people really want most is someone to listen to them. As the Bible says in the book of James, we are called to be "careful, thoughtful listener[s]."

The Bible says this for a reason: A big chunk of humility is learning to listen more than you talk. The reason so many of us are bad listeners today is that we are: a) in a hurry, and b) so self-centered that we think it's more important to tell others what *we're* thinking than to listen to what's on their mind.

Those of us who are striving to be more humble should be careful to avoid the habit of interrupting. When you interrupt someone, you are saying, "What I have to say is more important than what you are saying."

As a therapist, I've learned to listen more than I speak. That while some of my clients want to hear my pearls of wisdom, most are happier if I keep my trap closed for the lion's share of the session.

Listening to others is also a sign that you are not too full of pride to take someone else's point of view into consideration. This leads to the fifth and final lesson of death: Giving up your unhealthy sense of pride.

Exercise: Be mindful not to cut someone off when you're talking to them. Take time to really listen to someone else today.

THE LESSON OF CONTEMPLATING DEATH #5

Giving Up Our Unhealthy Sense Of Pride

PRIDE IS THE OPPOSITE OF HUMILITY. AND WHILE THERE IS "GOOD pride," which is a healthy respect for our selves and our accomplishments, the fact that we will one day pass away humbles us as it reminds us that we are only a part of a much bigger puzzle, right-sizing our egos in the process. Death shows us that, no matter how high we might climb in the social ladder, we will one day have to give up our status; that we are all alike in that we will all die. This section includes a spiritual gut-check, reminding us that we are not as spiritually advanced as we think. It introduces the law of humility and humiliation, and concludes with the path of not taking more credit than we deserve.

The Path Of Letting Go Of Pride

There's an Italian proverb that states, "Once the game is over, the king and the pawn go back in the same box." If death is a great teacher, this is the final lesson: That we shouldn't get too puffed up with pride, because death will take away whatever worldly status we've gained in the blink of an eye.

Humility is to pride as light is to darkness. The more humility you have the less pride you have and vice-versa. Ben Franklin found this out when he did an experiment to see how close he could come to living a perfect life. He mapped out all of the virtues he wanted to achieve and charted his progress—then abandoned the project when he discovered that the higher he scored on the other qualities, the lower he scored on humility! That said, there is such a thing as "good pride" (which we'll explore in the next section on Not Thinking Too Low of Ourselves), but I'm afraid most pride falls in the "bad pride" category as it stems from a lack of humility.

Pride is responsible for much of the misery in the world. How many wars were started because of pride? Nationalism, racial and religious pride are all dangerous in that they divide the human race into "us" against "them." On a more personal level, how many times have you or your spouse had to sleep on the couch because someone's pride acted up?

Not surprisingly, alcoholics anonymous has a lot to say about pride. On page 70 of *Twelve Steps and Twelve Traditions*, Bill Wilson writes:

> "The attainment of greater humility is the foundation principle of each of A.A.'s Twelve Steps...Humility, as a word and as an ideal, has a very bad time of it in our world. Not only is the idea misunderstood; the word itself is often intensely disliked...Much of the everyday

talk we hear, and a great deal of what we read, high-lights man's pride in his own achievements."

૨૭

Exercise: Humble yourself and let go of your unhealthy pride.

The Path Of Recognizing
We're Not Really That Spiritually Advanced

You may say, I'm a pretty good person. I have a right to be proud. In *Essential Teachings*, the Dalai Lama warns against following the "eight principals." These are: love of praise; rejection of blame; desiring gain; fearing loss; liking comfort and luxury; fearing discomfort and poverty; taking in all that is pleasant; rejecting all that is painful.

I don't know about you, but when I read that list of those things I'm supposed to avoid if I'm to reach spiritual maturity, I am deeply humbled.

ॐ

Exercise: Hold your life up to the above standard and humble yourself accordingly.

The Law Of Humility And Humiliation

P roverbs 16:18 states, "Pride goes before destruction, and a haughty spirit before a fall." This phrase summarizes the Law of Humility and Humiliation: that "a little humility will save you from a whole heap of humiliation." Back in the 1980s there was a commercial for the Fram oil filter. An auto mechanic came on the TV, holding up an oil filter and saying, "You can pay me now, or you can pay me later." That is, you can change your oil filter regularly or you can pay a whole lot more to have your engine fixed when it blows a gasket. The same thing works with humility. A little preventive maintenance—that is, a little humility—can save you a whole heap of humiliation later on. That's because when we don't humble ourselves, God has to do it for us. And that means humiliation.

The Bible is full of stories where pride comes before a fall. In fact, the Bible says that pride was the original sin because it caused Lucifer and 1/3rd of the angels to challenge God's authority, leading them to be cast down from heaven. Moreover, it could be argued that it was pride that caused the fall of man in the garden of Eden, when Adam and Eve ate from the tree God had told him not to instead of humbly submitting to God's will. This is a theme that is carried throughout the Bible, with the proud laid low and the humble exalted.

Look what happened to Pharaoh when he hardened his heart against the people of Israel, only to be drowned in the Red Sea. David was exalted by God when he was a humble servant, but when he counted the people of Israel in the book of Numbers to assess his own power, God humbled him as well.

Andrew Murray, in his classic *Humility: The Journey Toward Holiness* states, "Humility, the place of entire dependence on God, is from the very nature of things the first duty and the highest virtue of His creatures. And so pride—the loss of humility—is the root of every sin and evil." (p. 16) No wonder that, when Christians speak of the "seven deadly sins" pride comes first.

But you don't have to be a Christian to believe that pride comes before a fall. Look at the people who got so puffed up with pride that they wanted to take over the world. How did things work out for Hitler? For Mussolini? For Emperor Hirohito?

And I believe if you look at your own life, you will see how the same process has played out. How many people have you seen let their pride cause them to fall? How many times have you refused to bend out of pride and suffered for it? Conversely, how many times have you humbled yourself and been blessed? There's a good reason for this: People like and want to help humble folk and tend to resist the proud.

My Example: Learning Humility Through Humiliation

As someone who has had arrogance issues for five decades, my pride has gotten the best of me on numerous occasions. But two examples stick out.

In high school I was a hotshot tennis player who ruled the courts of Woods Hole, Massachusetts. Known as the port for the ferry to Martha's Vineyard, Woods Hole also hosts the Marine Biological Laboratory and the Woods Hole Oceanographic Institute. Back in the 1970s and 1980s, scientists from all over the world descended on Woods Hole every summer to work on squid axons.

Now scientists are an egotistical lot, and in Woods Hole there were two paths to the fame my father and his cohorts so desperately craved: Win the Woods Hole tennis tournament or, and this was a distant second, win a Nobel Prize. And while there were any number of Nobel Prize winners in Woods Hole, there was only one reigning Woods Hole tennis champion!

Blessed with scientist DNA, I did the math—and chose tennis. I practiced daily, and by the time I was 16 won The Tournament for the first of three consecutive times. I was so full of myself I lost all of my childhood friends. I remember thinking they all wanted to be me. Maybe it was true, but we didn't stay friends due to my insufferable pride (which showed itself off the tennis court as well). As reigning champion, I refused to play with two of my adult friends because they weren't good enough. When I finally gave in, we had a wonderful time. News flash: You don't have to be evenly matched to play tennis. You don't even have to play games. You can play *for fun!*

If my attitude as Woods Hole Tennis King was the height of *hubris* (ancient Greek for "a whole shipload of pride"), my lack of humility would reach its zenith in the mid-1990s as a teacher in the school made famous by the movie *Lean On Me.* Two weeks into the school year I would seal my fate with the following conversation between myself and a coworker in front of several other teachers at a local lunch dive:

Coworker: "Maybe if you're lucky Ms. P will give you a [the sex act that got President Bill Clinton impeached.]"

Me: "I wouldn't let her."

Coworker: "Because you're afraid she might bite?"

Me: "No, I just wouldn't *let* her."

That is, I was too young and pretty to *allow* my boss, who was overweight and no threat to Miss New Jersey, to do to me what others would have gladly paid her to do to them. Later I would learn that my teacher friend liked to complain about our boss to others then tell her everything they said.

Known as "Miss Piggy" to the students and "The Commandant" to her subordinates, Miss P (not her real letter) was tougher than a Roller Derby Queen on steroids, and those who worked under her and Principal Joe Clark swore she made the bat-wielding principal look tame. Miss P had a penchant for targeting one teacher per year, and my arrogance had painted a bright red bull's-eye on my handsome derriere. That year I got what I had coming—over and over again. My boss made my life a living hell, doing things like making me lower the first-quarter grades I'd already given my students because I'd violated a "school grading policy" that—surprise, surprise—did not exist. This led to death threats. My boss tried hard to get me fired and, failing that, gave me an evaluation which got me banned from teaching full-time in New Jersey public schools.

Not long after that, a woman I met while teaching at a Christian school in Newark told me "a hard head makes for a soft behind"—her way of saying God would humble me until I gave up my pride. I lost that job too, and God has been humbling me when I've failed to humble myself ever since.

In addition to my own testimony, I saw this truth played out in my family in the summer of 1983, when my ex-girlfriend, Ana, and I were staying in New Orleans with my mother and my great aunt and uncle. My great aunt Ethel acted as if she were the Queen of England and looked down on us the way royalty looks at peasants she reviles. Ana, who was Puerto Rican and proud of it, didn't appreciate it *at all.*

One night Ana and I came home late. To get to our bedroom we had to walk through the room where my great uncle and aunt Ethel were sleeping on a mattress on the floor. But when I got to the top of the stairs, I heard Ana make a strange noise. Something like a muffled sheep bleating.

Ana had made it across the room. She'd moved quickly, tip-toeing like a mouse, but I couldn't understand why. Then I looked down and realized why she'd moved so fast and what that weird bleating sound was. I looked at Ana and then looked down again, and realized ahead of me lay the most difficult twelve feet of my life.

For a moment I was caught like a deer in the headlights. On the other side of the room was Ana, her hand over her mouth to keep herself from laughing out loud. Right in front of me was the reason Ana was covering her mouth.

You can't tell me God doesn't have a sense of humor. For there before us were not one, but two of the barest bottoms known to man!

Somehow my great aunt and uncle had not only managed to wriggle out of their covers but their nighties as well!

Now all I had to do was to get to the other side of the room without bursting out laughing—a Herculean task with my girlfriend chortling to herself on the other side.

Somehow I made it across. When I got to the other side, Ana pulled me into our room, closed the door and began repeating the mantra that set off twenty minutes of uncontrollable laughter. "Two asses!" she said. "Two asses!"

God can and will humble the proud.

The Path Of Not Taking Credit

I start this path out with two quotations. The first one, by an unknown author states "There is no limit to what can be done if it doesn't matter who gets the credit."

The second, by Turkish preacher and Islamic scholar Muhammed Fethulla Gulen, is as follows:

"Self-conceit shows a lack of sensibility and maturity. Those who are more reflective and spiritually mature have the sense to attribute whatever gifts they may have to the Creator, the Most High, and devote themselves to him with humble gratitude."

I remember hearing former Washington Redskins football coach Joe Gibbs talking about how he prepared for a game. A religious Christian, Gibbs said he would stop and think about what he actually could take credit for apart from God. "Not much," he concluded. Another famous football coach, Alabama's Paul "Bear" Bryant, was known for his philosophy that, if someone made a mistake, the blame lay with Bryant, and if someone did something well, the credit was theirs.

One of the most important paths to humility is the path of not taking credit. There's something powerful in being able to do something well and letting someone else take the credit. This is especially true when that someone else is God.

Take this book for example. There are certain ideas I'm proud of. In particular I like the idea that there are two questions society has us thinking about constantly—"What can I get out of life, and am I getting enough?" and "What do other people think of me?"—and how this dilemma can be easily remedied by tweaking the two questions a bit (something we'll get to later).

Yet when I stop to think about where this inspiration came from, it is clear that it came from God and not myself. For who put that idea into my head in the first place? As for my modest talents as a writer, that, too, came from God/good genes, as all of our talents do.

Still, I might argue that the years I spent toiling on this book should count for something. I mean, don't we get credit for our perspiration even if we can't take credit for the inspiration?

Maybe. But when I stop to think about it, I realize that my work ethic was something that was not only in my genes (my father, my mother and my two grandfathers all accomplished more than me), it was based in large part on my upbringing.

Now you may be thinking, "By that logic, no one could take credit for anything."

Bingo.

This doesn't mean we can't be humbly grateful that God has used us—an example of the "good pride" we're about to explore in the upcoming section on not thinking too low of ourselves. What's more, the fact that you are not seeking the credit for something you did means you will be creating more good karma for yourself than you would if you had been seeking the credit, as God/the Universe will reward you for keeping your motives pure.

Isn't Life wonderful!

Exercise: Do something good today for which you will get no credit whatsoever.

Paths That Help Us
Not Think Too Low Of Ourselves

"Humility is the proper estimate of oneself."

— CHARLES SPURGEON

While humility is an important lesson for those of us who think too highly of ourselves, many of us have the opposite problem: We suffer from a low self-esteem that causes us to think negatively about ourselves.

While this may not seem to be a humility issue, it is, in that it involves thinking of oneself too much (albeit negatively). And as the above quotation from Charles Spurgeon states, humility is a "proper estimate of oneself," not a false humility that denies the value of our human existence. For as we'll see, we humans—and in particular we as humans who are striving to improve ourselves—have reason to be "appropriately proud" (to coin a term).

What's interesting is that, paradoxically, you can actually suffer from both an overinflated ego and poor self-esteem at the same time. In fact, this is the norm, not the exception, as a weak ego is one that feels the need to overinflate.

I was sitting with a former client of mine the other day discussing the outline for this book when he told me how great it was that I was including a section on not thinking too low of oneself. He reminded me that many people walk around thinking they aren't worth much and that thinking about themselves is wrong because it is "not humble."

Like many of us, Joe was told by someone in his family that he wasn't worth much, and that he shouldn't think too highly of himself because that was egotistical.

"I'm a good person," Joe said, tears welling up in his eyes. "I care about others. I look for opportunities to do good. I can look in a mirror and get a good feeling about myself without being a narcissist."

This was something I internalized myself, and I couldn't agree more. My father and I are now closer than ever, yet for much of my life he felt he had a duty to see to it that I didn't think too much of myself. When I aced him on the tennis court as a teenager and tried humbly to point out that I was actually aiming for the other side of the service box, he yelled at me and said I was "bragging." When I proceeded to win the local tennis tournament three times in a row, he threatened to charge me a $100 for playing in it the following year as he thought I was winning too much. This persisted into my 40's. When I told him one day that my Social Work professor said that I'd gotten the only 100 she'd ever given on the research final, his comment was "She must not have been teaching very long."

Ouch.

Now he's my biggest cheerleader. This shows how people and relationships can change over time—even when you think they never will. Interestingly, my client had a similar experience with his father, who had suddenly become very loving and affirming after putting Joe down for most of his life.

If you ever suffer from low self-esteem, the following paths will help put your life in perspective.

The Path Of Recognizing
You Are The Product Of A Champion Sperm
And A Precious Egg

You are a champion. You are the product of a champion sperm so successful it beat out up to 1.2 *billion* other sperm in the race to fertilize your mother's egg, one of millions your mother produces in a lifetime (of which about 500 will ovulate). And if the fact that you are the product of a one-in-a-billion sperm and a specially chosen egg isn't enough of a miracle for you (a birth that would not have happened at all if, for instance, your father had gotten up to get a glass of water), just do the math and you'll realize how miraculous your birth truly was. For as improbable as that may have been, for *your* miraculous birth to have occurred, both of your parents had to have been born the same miraculous way!

Now I'm not a math wizard, but it doesn't take Albert Einstein to figure out that this same improbable scenario had to play itself out over and over again, not just with your parents, but with all four of your grandparents, who had to meet at the exactly right time, with all eight of your great-grandparents, with all 16 of your great-great-grandparents, with all 32 of your great-great-great-grandparents, and so on into the unknowable past. That, in fact, if just ONE of your ancestors going back to the dawn of mankind had failed to follow the plan you would not be reading these words today.

Exercise: If you find yourself feeling down at any point today, remind yourself that you are a miracle. A one in a zillion product of a long line of champion sperm and special eggs. Then remind yourself that everyone you meet today is just such a champion as well—and treat them that way.

The Path Of Recognizing
You Are The Pinnacle Of Evolution

Buddhists in general and the Dalai Lama in particular talk about being thankful for our human birth as it affords us the opportunity to attain enlightenment. We humans take it for granted that we are at the top of the food chain, the most highly evolved species on the planet. We have all kinds of benefits that come from our ability to cooperate and share our gifts with one another. Our homes, our automobiles, our technology—even our clothes which are often made in other lands—are all examples of the benefits we 21st century humans enjoy.

From a scientific standpoint, you and I are the pinnacle of evolution. It took God/evolution billions of years to produce beings capable of the kind of introspection we alone seem capable of.

This ability came with a price. If humans can think like nobody's business, we also suffer like no other species on Earth. War, torture, and the ability to inflict physical, mental and emotional distress on others are a direct consequence of our free will. Whether we're suffering from the anxiety produced by an overactive brain, or at the hands of an evil person who is intent on causing us harm, there is little doubt that human suffering can be worse than anything the other animals on the planet may face.

As we've seen in the previous section, this is why death is such a blessing. That, in a world with no death, nothing would keep some of us from torturing others for an eternity.

❧

Exercise: Think of the 13 plus billion years it took God to create the universe and put humans on this earth. Reflect on the fact that you are the result of evolution.

The Path Of Recognizing
You Are The Center Of God's Creation

Matthew 10:29-31 states: "Are not two sparrows sold for a farthing? and one of them shall not fall on the ground without your Father. But the very hairs of your head are all numbered. Fear ye not therefore, ye are of more value than many sparrows."

Not only can humans savor and devise greater earthly pleasures than other creatures, our ability to think at a higher level makes us capable of worshipping (and, in some cases, rejecting) a Higher Power.

We've already seen how we are the pinnacle of evolution. Now let's focus on how important we are to the God of the Universe. The Bible says He has numbered the very hairs on our head. That means He knows so much about us that not one detail of who we are is lost to Him. As we discussed in The Path of How Little We Know Ourselves, God knows us MUCH better than we know ourselves, as only He has access to our potential and knows the hidden depths of our unconscious.

The Bible also says that we are the pinnacle of creation. That God created humankind in His image on the sixth day of creation. God wrote the Bible through humans and for humans. That in itself speaks volumes about how much He loves us. As does the fact that He sent down His only begotten Son to die on a cross for us so that we could be forgiven for our sins. To say nothing of the gift of the Holy Spirit which is available to no other creature on this Earth.

Of course we also suffer in ways that no other species does. Our ability to choose to worship God also affords us the opportunity to reject Him. And without a proper sense of humility, our self-consciousness can cause us to suffer unnecessarily.

❧

Exercise: Remind yourself how much God loves you. Reflect on the fact that you are His child and that He is your Father.

The Path Of Recognizing Your Worth To Others

Sometimes when you're feeling low it's a good idea to stop and think about how important you are to the people in your life. Think about your friends and family. Those who count on you at work or in your place of worship. As important as the fearless moral inventory we did in Section II, where we took a good hard look at our shortcomings and realized how far from perfect we were, it is equally important to recognize the good in us as well. If you are having a hard time with this, ask someone who cares about you what they value in you. Also, if you have children you love, try to look at yourself the way you look at your son or daughter.

Of course we will never know this side of the grave all of the ways our lives have blessed others. That's okay. For now, just think of some of the ways you have been a blessing and be grateful that God/The Universe has given you the opportunity to do some good—and that you can enjoy the good feeling that comes from recognizing your worth to others.

Exercise: Write down some of the things you've done for others or that others have told you you've done for them. Look at this list every time your self-esteem needs a boost.

PATH TO HUMILITY #48

_____

The Path Of Looking At Ourselves
As Glasses That Are Half Full

I often tell my psychotherapy clients about the importance of looking at the circumstances and people in their lives as glasses that are half full rather than half empty. (For whatever reason, most of my clients complain about others more than they complain about themselves.)

However, it is just as important to remember that we need to look at ourselves with the same compassion we try to show others. Here it's important to remind ourselves that, while we might not be all we ought to be, we are undoubtedly better than what we could be.

Nobody's perfect, and if you're always looking at your flaws and not your strengths, you are bound to feel guilty and depressed. You are a child of the universe, someone who deserves to be loved. You have many fine qualities and have done many good things. In fact, you care so much about being a loving human being you are reading a book on humility so that you can become even more humble and loving than you are now. Yes, you are a work in progress, but remember, so is everyone else.

℘

Exercise: Just as the previous challenge was to write down what you've done for others, this time I'd like you to make a list of your good qualities and accomplishments. If you can't think of any (and, yes, I've actually had clients who said they can't think of a single positive about themselves), ask a friend or a loved one to help you out. Then read it back to yourself when you need a boost—or read the following poem by Max Ehrmann.

Desiderata

Go placidly amid the noise and haste,
and remember what peace there may be in silence.
As far as possible without surrender be on good terms with all persons.
Speak your truth quietly and clearly; and listen to others,
even the dull and the ignorant; they too have their story.
Avoid loud and aggressive persons, they are vexations to the spirit.
If you compare yourself with others, you may become vain and bitter;
for always there will be greater and lesser persons than yourself. Enjoy
your achievements as well as your plans.
Keep interested in your own career, however humble;
it is a real possession in the changing fortunes of time.
Exercise caution in your business affairs;
for the world is full of trickery.
But let this not blind you to what virtue there is;
many persons strive for high ideals;
and everywhere life is full of heroism.
Be yourself.
Especially, do not feign affection.
Neither be cynical about love;
for in the face of all aridity and disenchantment
it is as perennial as the grass.
Take kindly the counsel of the years,
gracefully surrendering the things of youth.
Nurture strength of spirit to shield you in sudden misfortune.
But do not distress yourself with dark imaginings.
Many fears are born of fatigue and loneliness.
Beyond a wholesome discipline,
be gentle with yourself.
You are a child of the universe,
no less than the trees and the stars; you have a right to be here.

And whether or not it is clear to you,
no doubt the universe is unfolding as it should.
Therefore be at peace with God, whatever you conceive Him to be,
and whatever your labors and aspirations,
in the noisy confusion of life keep peace with your soul.
With all its sham, drudgery, and broken dreams,
it is still a beautiful world.
Be cheerful.
Strive to be happy.

Max Ehrmann, Desiderata

Paths That Help Us Not Think Of Ourselves Too Often

"Your inner growth is completely dependent upon the realization
that the only way to find peace and contentment is
to stop thinking about yourself."

— Michael Singer, *The Untethered Soul*

"Humility is not thinking less of yourself,
it's thinking about yourself less."

—Rick Warren, *The Purpose Driven Life*

Humility is not just putting ourselves in perspective by not thinking too highly or too low of ourselves. As every self-aholic knows, humility also means thinking about ourselves less often. It's no coincidence that this section begins with a quote oft repeated in A.A. meetings.

In fact, it could be argued that our constant thinking about ourselves—even more than thinking too highly or too low of ourselves—is the main reason 21st century humankind has become a race of self-aholics. That thinking too often about ourselves is THE main problem we face today. For as we've seen we live in a self-obsessing society. A society that has turned us into neurotic basket cases who are constantly thinking about what we can get out of life and what other people think of us.

A society that has forgotten what Copernicus taught us 400 years ago—that the world does not revolve around us. A society so self-obsessed we even have a popular magazine named *Self*. A society that has made self-aholics of virtually every one of us.

This is not our fault. At least not entirely.

For not only do we live in a society which is constantly bombarding us with messages about the importance of looking out for Number One, we each have a little voice inside our heads doing the exact same thing!

Fortunately, the self-consciousness and self-ishness that makes us so anxious and/or selfish today can be alleviated (if not completely cured) by the paths in this section. Paths which help us shatter the "room full of mirrors" in which we live, allowing us to see with childlike wonder the beautiful dance that is Life. Paths which help us to remember that we are but a part of this world, not its center.

That, as the title of this book suggests, it's not all about us.

SUBSECTION A

Three Paths Of Realistic Expectations

The following paths help us right-size our expectations about Life the same way this book as a whole right-sizes our perception of ourselves. They are designed to help us stop having the unrealistic expectations that make us so neurotic, selfish and depressed.

The Path Of Recognizing
Our Wants Are Not Our Needs

As we've seen, we live in a society that encourages us to believe that it is, in fact, all about us. A world where our wants have become our needs, leading us to act as if we can't survive without the material blessings we crave. As we just noted, this is not your fault. We have been conditioned like rats on a treadmill, to believe we *need* the newest cell phone, the luxury car, the choicest real estate, etc.

Equating our wants with our needs makes us particularly susceptible to selfishness and worry, as any of our "needs" that go unmet are taken way out of proportion. This extends to all of the little ways in which we tell ourselves our lives should go. We want everyone to like us and everything to go our way, and when it doesn't happen—or even when we are merely afraid that it *might* not happen—we get anxious, which can lead to selfishness or depression.

❧

Exercise: Pay attention to your anxiety. Then ask yourself if the anxiety is coming from treating something you want as if it were something you need. Remind yourself that your wants are not your needs.

The Path Of Expecting Less And Getting More

There was a period of several years in my life when I was plagued by social anxiety attacks that came from being so self-conscious I literally "freaked out." While no one else could see how bad I was feeling on the inside, I felt as if everyone was watching me and I had to hold it together so that they wouldn't see that I was having a nervous breakdown.

In desperation I turned to a 15 CD course by the Midwest Center called "Attacking Anxiety and Depression." And whether it was due to the 14 CDs of cognitive behavioral therapy, or the relaxation CD I listened to daily, the social anxiety attacks stopped after using the program for several months.

What was interesting about the course was that the one CD that didn't impress me when I first listened to it was the one the program said I wouldn't be so enthused about at the time but would remember in the future. That CD was called "expecting less and getting more." And while for the life of me I cannot remember the names of any of the other CDs, this one stays in my mind.

The CD taught me that lowering my expectations of myself, others and Life in general allowed me to appreciate them without needing them to be perfect. I remember the program's creator, Lucinda Bassett, talking about how she was able to enjoy a vacation even when it rained every day. This was all about being humbly grateful (for the vacation) instead of grumbly hateful (because the weather was lousy). It also relates to the importance of remembering the difference between our wants and our needs, and speaks to the following path of not expecting heaven on Earth.

❧

Exercise: Lower your unrealistic expectations about life and be humbly grateful for all of the blessings you receive.

The Path Of Not Expecting Heaven On Earth

B en Franklin said he liked to expect the worst so that he would be pleasantly surprised when things didn't go so badly.

We moderns could use to be a little more Franklin.

One of the unspoken myths we have today is that we can have heaven on Earth. That the sensual pleasures, material blessings and the diversions created by our vast entertainment industry can make our lives so enjoyable we will be happy all the time.

This, we know, is nonsense. After all, there are some folks in Third World countries living in mud-thatched huts with no shoes on their feet who are happy despite their poverty, while there are millionaires and billionaires so miserable they commit suicide, either slowly by poisoning themselves with drugs and alcohol, or actually killing themselves outright.

But there's another claim which is more complicated. That disciplining our minds can make our earthly existence heavenly. This claim deserves more careful thought, as it speaks to the limits of humility.

While it is clear that having a greater appreciation for everything in your life will make you happy with less, that it will help you get through tragedies that would destroy a weaker person, there *is* a limit to what humility can do for us.

For while a disciplined, humble mind can handle all kinds of psychological stress, excruciating physical pain feels terrible no matter who you are. When I'm really sick all I want is to feel better, and when I told my former pastor I couldn't pray when I was sick, she said that was how it is for all of us. What about those suffering from PTSD who are having nightmares they can't control? Or someone with a mental illness who is going out of their minds?

Worse yet, what if you are one of those unfortunate people who are being tortured—or, God forbid, being forced to watch your children being tortured?

The bottom line is that there is evil in this world. And whether you chalk it up to Satan or a combination of original sin and bad karma, we ultimately have to reconcile ourselves to the fact that we live in a world riddled with pain and unhappiness. A world where tens of millions died in two world wars. A world where 6 million Jews were exterminated in Nazi Germany. A world where the ancestors of African Americans suffered the horrors of two hundred years of slavery and another two hundred years of inequality. A world where, according to Amnesty International, torture is being used in over 130 countries.

Rather than depressing us, however, we can recognize that: 1) the VAST majority of the pain we experience comes from our inability to be humbly grateful rather than grumbly hateful (our inability to appreciate the good in life instead of being upset about the bad); and 2) that we can hope for a more heavenly existence in the next world. Plus there's the interesting paradox that we can make our own existence more heavenly by *not* expecting heaven on Earth and being humbly grateful for the blessings we *do* receive, knowing that there will be some struggles along the way. Furthermore, recognizing that there are others who have it worse than us, whether because they are less humbly grateful than ourselves or are simply going through a tough time in their lives, can give us more compassion—a quality the Dalai Lama says is the key to happiness.

In *The Untethered Soul* Michael Singer says that while pain is the universal language of the body, fear is the universal language of the psyche. As we've just discussed, there is a limit to what humility can do for those of us in physical pain. But Singer argues that we can, with enough spiritual growth (or, as I would put it, with enough humility), live a life completely devoid of fear.

While I'm not sure we can keep fear away for good in a fallen world, I have noticed that the more humble and spiritually grounded I become, the more often I feel no anxiety at all. So if Singer, who is a spiritual teacher where I am but a student, says I can live a life without fear of any kind, I'm happy to shoot for that.

Exercise: If you've been expecting heaven on earth, right-size your expectations about life on planet earth. Instead of being bitter that life is not perfect, be grateful for all of the positive experiences you have.

Paths That Take the Focus Off Of Ourselves By Not Thinking About Self

"One cannot be humble
and aware of oneself at the same time."

— Madeleine L'Engle, *A Circle of Quiet*

The Path Of Letting Go
Of The Melodrama Of The Mind

S inger says that the first step to letting go of the melodrama your mind creates is recognizing that you are not the voice inside your head. He points out that you cannot BE the voice because you are the one who hears it. Likewise, you cannot BE your emotions because you are the one who feels them. And that you cannot BE your body because you are the one who experiences the sensations from a body that has been changing since you were conceived. What you are is the Consciousness that experiences your thoughts, emotions and physical sensations.

Once you've recognized you are not the voice in your head, you are in a position to see how neurotic that voice truly is, and how it is constantly giving you bad advice. That it is almost never satisfied and can have a problem with just about everything. That it is the voice that makes you believe life is all about you when it really isn't.

In *The Untethered Soul*, Singer states that, "You will realize the only price you have to pay is letting go of yourself." While he is right, of course, this is actually quite a high price to pay for us self-aholics!

Exercise: Recognize that you are not the voice in your head or your feelings; that you are the one who hears these thoughts and feels these emotions. If you have the time, read *The Untethered Soul*.

The Path Of Giving Up
The Part Of You That Needs Protecting

S inger goes on to say that a healthy psyche, like a healthy body, isn't aware of itself, and that you will never be psychologically healthy until you give up trying to protect yourself.

Giving up your need to defend yourself is very difficult, for we live in a society where unhealthy psyches are the rule, not the exception. A society where we have become a race of self-aholics who believe it's all about us.

On page 61 of the *Untethered Soul*, Singer says that "real spiritual growth happens when there is only one of you inside. There's not a part that's scared and another part that's protecting the part that's scared. All parts are unified." He says that this can be accomplished by constantly reminding yourself that you are the one who *notices* the voice inside your head screaming for protection and scheming for ways to protect yourself. I believe humility also keeps you from being divided between the part of you that's scared and the part that's protecting that part, as it helps you accept life as it is, allowing you to live without fear of life's events.

Exercise: Use your humility to keep from fighting life today. Instead of being two people—the self who needs protection and the one who is protecting your self-image—allow yourself just to experience life with gratitude, not worrying about having to defend yourself at all. Allow yourself the freedom just to accept life as it comes.

The Path Of Thinking About How Events Are Good For Others Instead Of How They Affect You

William Temple once wrote: "Humility does not mean thinking less of yourself than of other people, nor does it mean having a low opinion of your own gifts. It means freedom from thinking about yourself at all."

Those of us who are self-aholics are constantly worried about how our own and other people's actions affect us. We base our decisions on how to deal with situations and other people on what we calculate will bring us the maximum benefit. We are repeatedly asking ourselves "How will this affect me?" When we stop focusing on ourselves and think about how our actions will affect others (or please our Higher Power) rather than worrying about how they will affect us—we are on the road to a healthier psyche and a holier life.

When we become other- and God-focused, we transcend our need to have Life revolve around us and we discover anew the plentiful blessings which God/The Universe has showered upon us. Blessings we were blind to when we were caught up in self. That's because when you are living under the tyranny of self, you are caught up with worrying about your "problems" (which, when properly viewed, are "challenges") and how to make everything and everybody in your world line up with the way you want them to go. All of this self-centeredness leads not to happiness, but unhappiness, as we fight the flow of Life and try to make it fit our needs and wants.

Thankfully, humility solves this problem for us, giving us the freedom to stop obsessing about ourselves. As the quotation above reminds us, "Humility does not mean thinking less of yourself than of other people, nor does it mean having a low opinion of your own gifts. It means freedom from thinking about yourself at all."

☙

Exercise: Think about those areas of your life where you've let "self" creep in. Now go through your day staying other- and God-focused, applying the humility that allows you not to think of yourself at all.

The Path Of Renouncing
The Little Mafioso In Your Head

I don't know about you, but I have a little Mafioso in my head who pops up from time to time to tell me that I need to do "this to that one," "that to this one"—and why I should make so-and-so sleep with the fishes.

Closely related to the previous path, we all have our current "enemies list" and how we plan to exact revenge—or, at least, "put them in their place."

My little Mafioso shows up a lot when I'm on the road and I see someone driving inconsiderately, either zig-zagging in and out of traffic or failing to properly alternate merge.

It is then that the word "A—hole" pops into my still-not-so-sanctified head. Utilizing the Path of I Used To Be Disgusted But Now I Try To Be Amused, I think to myself how fun it would be to treat A—hole's like foreigners or people from another planet. You know, the way you would treat a person who you suddenly realized was handicapped. I imagine myself talking to the person in this manner: "Oh, I'm sorry, pardon me, I didn't realize you were an A—hole (or from the planet "A—holius"). Please forgive me for getting upset with you. Have a nice day."

This is my version of road rage.

Exercise: The next time the little Mafioso in your head pops up, remind yourself of the following three quotes which I've mentioned earlier in this book but are worth repeating:

"Of some thoughts one stands perplexed—especially
at the sight of men's sin—and wonders whether one
should use force or humble love. Always decide to use
humble love. If you resolve on that, once and for all,
you may subdue the whole world. Loving humility is
marvelously strong, and strongest of all things, and
there is nothing else like it."

— FYODOR DOSTOYEVSKY

"Humility is a willingness to be underestimated
or slighted and feel no resentment."
— PETER WAGNER

"O Lord, Remember not only the men and women of
good will but all those of ill will. But do not remember
all the suffering they have inflicted upon us; remember
the fruits we have bought thanks to this suffering—our
comradeship, our loyalty, our humility, our courage,
our generosity, the greatness of heart which has grown
out of all this; and when they come to judgment, let
all the fruits we have borne be their forgiveness."

— FOUND IN CONCENTRATION CAMP
FOR WOMEN PRISONERS IN NAZI GERMANY

The Path Of Recognizing Others
Are More Worried About What You Think Of Them Than
They Are Busy Judging You

My primary care physician once pointed out to me something none of my psychotherapists ever did. He said that when you walk into a room full of people, they aren't thinking so much about you, as they are focused on what others (including you) are thinking of them.

Be mindful that you are not the center of anyone else's universe, as others are more concerned about their own worlds than they are with you. This simple practice can alleviate a lot of unnecessary worry when it comes to dealing with people, especially with those with whom you do not have a close relationship.

This path is particularly useful when going to a social occasion where you are worried about how you're coming across to others. Simply remind yourself that they are more worried about how they're coming across than focusing on you.

If you still feel nervous, do what they tell people with stage fright to do: Pretend everyone else is walking around in their underwear.

☙

Exercise: The next time you find yourself uncomfortable at a social event, remind yourself that everyone else is more focused on what folks are thinking about them than they are focused on you.

The Path Of Not Worrying About Yourself

Mark Twain once wrote "I'm an old man and have known many troubles, but most of them never happened."

One of my favorite exchanges from the show *Game of Thrones* was when Robb Stark asked his father, Ned Stark, "How can I be brave when I'm so afraid?"

To which Ned replies: "That's the only time a man can be brave."

The greatest blessing humility has to offer you is the freedom to stop worrying about yourself. Essentially this is what *It's Not all About You!* is all about. For not thinking too highly of oneself, not thinking too low of oneself and thinking of oneself less often all help us take the focus off of our neurotic selves.

I've found that reading and re-reading the Bible and *The Untethered Soul* have been profoundly helpful. In particular, I've found the following quotes in today's "Exercise" to be extremely helpful whenever I'm tempted to worry. I suggest you turn to them when worry comes your way.

છ

Exercise: Remember the following quotes whenever you are feeling tempted to worry:

"A man goes to knowledge as a man goes to war:
Wide awake, with fear, with respect and with absolute assurance."

— CARLOS CASTENEDA, *THE TEACHINGS OF DON JUAN*

"If you're bothered by the future,
you're making up a future that doesn't exist that bothers you."

— MICHAEL SINGER

"Everything will be okay as soon as you are okay with everything—
and that's the only time everything will be okay."

— MICHAEL SINGER

"All things work together for good to them that love God,
to those who are the called according to His purpose."

— ROMANS 8:28

"For God has not given us the spirit of fear,
but of power, and of love, and of a sound mind."

— 2 TIMOTHY 1:7

SUBSECTION C

Paths That Bless Others

O nce we give up our unnecessary worry, we are free to focus on paths that bless others and bless God. Paths that help us take our minds off of ourselves as they help others at the same time. Like the paths in the beginning of Section II, they will not only benefit your mental health, they will improve your relations with your fellow human beings.

The Path Of Thinking Of Others' Needs
As Well As Our Own

I'm a terrible grocery shopper. I'll go and get everything I need and not think about what my wife and son want. At least that's what I used to do until my wife called it to my attention. Now don't get me wrong, I'm not a deadbeat husband/dad. I am always careful to pick up the necessities my family needs (milk and cereal for my growing son, etc.), and when my wife or son asks me to get them food, I do. It's just that left to my own devices I will focus more on my own needs than my family's.

While some people naturally think of others as well as themselves (I've heard some say they think of others' needs *more* than their own), it doesn't come so naturally to me. Maybe that's why I wrote this book—so I could read it and get over myself!

When we focus on what others need from us instead of what we need from them, we take the focus off of ourselves. Being other-focused is the key to avoiding the anxiety that comes with trying to make everything work out for our good. When you are me-focused, anything that might get in the way of our happiness becomes something to worry about. However, when you switch the focus off of self to how we can benefit others, we lose all of that self-conscious worry.

Exercise: Focus on what others around you want and/or need from you today, thinking of how much good you can do for others in the next 24 hours.

The Path Of Being Nice To Others

While I don't do so well about thinking of others' needs before my own, I am usually good about being nice. I wasn't always so. And my mother has many stories of what a schmuck I was as a teenager (stories about things I've done that I never remember). At work I am known as "the gum man" because I always bring a pack of gum to share with my co-workers and clients at the homeless shelter where I work part-time. I enjoy being friendly to others and it pays off, both in business terms, as the case managers are eager to refer clients my way—clients who keep coming back in part because I am nice to them as well—and in the good feeling I get of having others like me which makes my work much more enjoyable.

You've heard the saying "nice guys finish last." Well, it's just not true.

Studies show that: 1) Nice people make more money. A Rutgers University study showed that each 2 percent of cheerfulness in an organization's employees translated into a 1 percent increase in profits for the company. Furthermore, people like nice people and want to help them, helping them move up the ladder more quickly. 2) Nice people live longer. People who volunteer their time tend to live longer than those who don't, and being nice creates less stress leading to better health outcomes, 3) Nice people have happier love lives and are 50 percent less likely to divorce than the rest of the population. 4) Nice people tend to be sued less and stay out of jail as they don't get into conflicts.

Anecdotally, I have a friend from grade school who was reasonably intelligent but not necessarily more book smart than myself and some of my other friends. Yet the thing about my friend was he was very nice and because of that had many friends of his own. I remember not playing with him out of pride because he had to "schedule me in" because he had so many play dates set up in 6th grade! Anyway, he wound up being a super-successful businessman and came very close to becoming the governor of Connecticut on his first try.

Exercise: Go out of your way to do something nice for someone else, and make a point of complimenting someone at work or at home.

The Path Of Serving Others

Bengali poet Rabindranath Tagore once wrote "I slept and dreamt that life was joy. I awoke and saw that life was service. I acted and behold, service was joy."

And then there is this passage from the 13th chapter of the gospel of John:

> "After that he poureth water into a bason, and began to wash the disciples' feet, and to wipe them with the towel wherewith he was girded....So after he had washed their feet, and had taken his garments, and was set down again, he said unto them, Know ye what I have done to you? Ye call me Master and Lord: and ye say well; for so I am. If I then, your Lord and Master, have washed your feet; ye also ought to wash one another's feet. For I have given you an example, that ye should do as I have done to you."

One of the most powerful paths to humility is to perform some humble act of self-sacrifice. In her excellent book *God Never Blinks*, Regina Brett talks about a friend of hers whose motto was "I get to" instead of "I have to." In other words, whenever her friend had to do something, he saw it as an opportunity instead of a hassle. "I get to take out the trash." "I get to wash the dishes." etc.

When we go out of our way to serve others instead of looking to be served, we change our focus from self-indulgence to helping our fellow human beings. Not only does this benefit them, it helps us greatly. For, like The Path of Thinking About How Events Are Good for Others Instead of How They Affect You, it helps us shift the focus away from that Tyrant, King Self. While the main focus of this book is about changing our mentality, this shift will manifest itself in how we act as well as think. By taking action to help someone else, we take our humility to the next level. As the Dalai Lama says in his book *Essential Teachings*, "Infantile people think only of their own comfort. Buddha works only for the good of others."

Perhaps the best known example of serving others comes in the New Testament. In the thirteenth chapter of the book of John, Jesus makes a point of washing the disciples' feet as an example of what they should do when He is gone. For Christians, lowering oneself to the level of a humble servant means rising higher in the kingdom, as Jesus said that in His kingdom the servant is greatest, flipping the values of our earthly kingdoms on their head. Society tells us that the masters are greater than the servants. Christ reminds us that in His kingdom it is the other way around. For Christians humility is not merely a form of meditation, but requires action.

Back in Bible times, foot washing was a necessity. The streets were dusty and folk walked around in sandals without socks or stockings. So washing them meant getting their hands dirty. Wives often washed their husband's feet. Children washed their parents' feet. Servants washed their masters' feet. For Jesus to wash the disciples' feet was a profound role-reversal. This was apparently too much for Peter, who responded by telling Jesus "Thou shalt never wash my feet." (Peter later changes his mind after Jesus admonishes him, asking Jesus to wash him from head to toe).

Jesus tells the disciples He is washing their feet as an "example," a word which is translated from the Greek *hypodeigma* which means "pattern." Jesus wasn't concerned about foot fungus or shiny toenails. It was the inner humility required to get down and dirty that He was highlighting. Humbling oneself in this way may not seem attractive to us, but it will be rewarded with the kind of inner peace that passes all understanding.

Exercise: "Wash someone's feet" today by serving them in whatever way you can find.

The Path Of Seeking To Give More Than You Get

"Lord, grant that I may seek rather to comfort than to be comforted—
to understand than to be understood—to love, than to be loved.
For it is by self-forgetting that one finds. It is by forgiving that one is
forgiven. It is by dying that one awakens to Eternal Life. Amen."

—The Prayer of St. Francis, excerpt

We've already discussed the related paths of Thinking About Others, Being Nice and Serving Others. All of these are related to the path of seeking to give more than we get. Looking closely at the Prayer of St. Francis, we see the blueprint for how humility shifts our focus off of ourselves on to how we can be a blessing to others. In so doing, we alleviate all of the negatives that come with our self-obsession. All of the worry, all of the anxiety, all of the selfishness slides away as we change our focus to blessing others instead of seeking to be blessed by them.

This reveals the answer to how to change the first question Society has us asking ourselves into something much more positive. Instead of asking ourselves "What can I GET out of life—and am I GETTING enough?" we should be asking ourselves "What can I GIVE to life—and am I GIVING enough?

This does not actually have to be an either/or situation, as I like to find ways where my giving and my getting overlap. For while it's true that by giving pleasure you will get pleasure, it doesn't mean you have to sacrifice everything that makes you happy in order to give happiness to someone else. That would be a form of masochism. So while there are times we have to turn off our favorite team's football game to listen to our wives (or, conversely, times we have to let our husbands watch their favorite team play instead of listening to us), and times we have to visit a sick relative instead of something we'd rather be doing, many times we can find things to do that both give us happiness and give others joy.

Changing our focus to "giving" as well as "getting" challenges us to be the best human beings we can instead of the most selfish version of ourselves—the one encouraged by asking only what we can GET out of life.

My uncle Ben Zion Cohen is a Lubovitch Rabbi in Israel. You've seen his counterparts in America, the Jews with the black suits and black hats.

While we've followed different spiritual paths, I admire his wisdom when it comes to marriage. Benny tells me that there are virtually no divorces among the men and women in his community. That, he says, is because the bride and groom are asked to look at marriage in terms of what can they *give* the other person rather that what they can *get* out of the relationship. While I recognize that there are other factors at play here, imagine how much better *our* marriages would be if our focus was on what we could give our mates instead of the "am I getting enough?"

And if the shift in focus from getting to giving could heal our marriages, imagine what it could mean for the rest of our lives? Truly, it would revolutionize our society. We'd walk around looking to be a blessing to others instead of looking to be blessed. To paraphrase President Kennedy, "Ask not what others can do for you, ask what you can do for others."

The Prayer of St. Francis also hints at how to transform the second question Society has us asking ourselves: "What do other people think of me?" St. Francis' prayer ends by talking about Eternal Life—it is, after all, a prayer written by a saint—which indicates that it was not only about pleasing others, but pleasing God as well. Now let's see how this relates to that question as we conclude *It's* Not *all About You!* with The Eight Paths of Blessing God.

❦

Exercise: Look at your schedule for the next week and see where you can give more than you get. Where you can put others' needs above yours—or where you can meet someone else's needs in a way that blesses you as well.

SUBSECTION D

The Path Of Believing In God
And The Eight Paths Of Blessing God

D ear reader, as we conclude, we come to the point where we have to have a serious talk about God. For while I have done what I could to make non-believers comfortable with my writing thus far, I feel it is important to have a discussion of belief in God (briefly exploring the reasons why some don't believe, why some do, and what are the benefits of believing), before concluding the book with seven paths to bless our Higher Power (and in so doing benefit ourselves).

While it is fairly obvious how my "believing" readers will benefit from these paths to humility, my hope is that those of you who are atheists will benefit as well and that, having come this far, you will stick it out to the end.

Some reasons to press on: First, this last section reveals how to transform the second question society has us asking ourselves ("What do other people think of me?") into something much more positive. Second, it will lead to a deeper understanding of how your believing brothers and sisters think.

And third, you might come to consider believing as an option you'd like to explore.

The Path Of Believing In God

As we've discussed previously, you don't have to believe in God to be humble or to benefit from the paths to humility outlined in this book. That said, belief in a Higher Power is itself a path of humility as it recognizes there is something greater than ourselves. It also helps solve the problem of putting ourselves in the center of the universe where no mortal –or even race of mortals—belongs. Only God can be the center of the Universe, as only God is Eternal.

Why Some Don't Believe

There are many reasons people don't believe in God. One of them is that they don't want to humble themselves and recognize that there is a Being greater than themselves. Others don't believe because they think mankind can answer all of his questions through reason alone. Another reason people don't turn to God is that they don't want anyone telling them how to live their lives. That is, they feel if they believe in God it will mean that they have to change their behavior.

Yet another reason people have for not believing is that they've had difficulties in their lives where they've been hurt by someone or suffered some devastating setback and can't understand why a loving, all powerful God would allow them to be hurt so much. Others see all of the evil in the world and decide that it is impossible to believe in such a God.

You may have grown up in a family like mine that didn't believe in God.

Or you may have stopped believing despite growing up in a family that *did* believe, perhaps because of what they taught you in college. Or maybe you had an absentee father or one who was abusive, making the idea of a loving, heavenly Father hard to accept. You may have been a victim of sexual perversion by clergy, or just been turned off by what you heard about such perversion. Maybe you didn't like church policies, such as their treatment of gay and lesbians. Or you knew some religious people who were hypocrites. Or some other reason I failed to mention.

I once believed that I could answer the age-old question of why an all powerful God would allow suffering. I was going to write a book on the subject where I would point out how suffering builds character, how it helps us relate to others who are suffering, and how it helps us appreciate Christ's sacrifice for us. Then I realized that this was only true of *limited* suffering.

What about the mother or father whose child is dying of leukemia? Or what if you are that child? What if you are someone in a third-world country who's starving or being tortured? What of slavery? The horrors of war and genocide? When I pondered these questions, I came to realize that there was some suffering so awful it didn't seem to have any purpose at all.

Christians and Jews explain evil in terms of free will (that is, we have been given the freedom to choose evil over good) and Satan who tempts men to do evil and is responsible for all of the suffering in the world. Islam views evil as beginning with Satan's refusal to bow down to Adam as commanded by Allah, for which he is cursed and sent out of heaven, and vows to get revenge by spending eternity tempting humans to do evil. Hindus and Buddhists ascribe suffering to karma. That said, if you're holding out on God because you can't reconcile an all powerful being with the evil you've experienced or know others suffer from, or from any other rational reasons, I encourage you to look into the book *The Reason for God* by Pastor Timothy Keller. In it Pastor Keller points out that just because we don't understand the reasons for suffering, doesn't mean that they don't exist.

In his book Pastor Keller also tackles the complaint expressed by many nonbelievers that there have been many atrocities committed in the name of religion. Here Keller points out that many non-religious political systems have been just as brutal, if not more so. What's more, the great writer and Trappist monk Thomas Merton pointed out that, for all we know, the only reason the human race is still on the planet is because of the prayers of the saints.

Finally, Pastor Keller points out that those who claim to have no beliefs whatsoever, actually have faith in their own belief system.

Why Some Of Us Believe

Some of the reasons to believe God exists include the beauty of Nature and all of the order in the universe that speaks to an intelligent Designer. While it may be accepted that the physical universe started with a big bang some 14 billion years ago, it begs the question, what existed *before* the big bang? There are other arguments as well, such as the "fine-tuning" argument found in Keller's book that discusses how the Earth had to be the perfect distance from the Sun to sustain life, etc.

While no rational argument can PROVE God exists, I'm reminded of the story I heard about a man who was listening to an atheist giving a talk about why he believed God/Jesus didn't exist.

The man in the back of the room listened attentively, then raised his right hand while eating an apple with his left.

"I have one question," he said between bites. "Tell me, sir, is the apple I just bit sour or sweet?"

When the speaker complained that there was no way he could know that, as he hadn't tasted the apple himself, the old man in the back replied. "You haven't tasted my Jesus either, and I have and can tell you, He's sweet."

This, essentially, is my answer to my atheist readers: I have tasted God, Jesus and the Holy Spirit and have found them to be sweeter than anything else on this Earth.

While I was once an atheist, I now see evidence of God everywhere. But as to why God doesn't just reveal Himself to everyone the way He has to me, I cannot say, though I suspect it has something to do with how hard I was seeking Him and how disturbed I was at the thought of my mortality.

Some Advantages Of Belief In God

As we've discussed, I almost had a nervous breakdown until God revealed to me that I was a Spirit that would live on long after Daniel Cohen died, and that God Himself was very real. So I know how disturbing it can be not to believe in God.

I also know how nice it is to have some faith. For there are many advantages to believing in God. First there is our own immortality to consider. For it is hard to imagine believing in an eternal soul, that is, Eternal Life, if there is no God.

Next comes the possibility of an eternal heaven and hell (or even a non-eternal one—for if hell exists I wouldn't want to spend *any* time there). This reminds me of Pascal's wager. In his book *Pensees*, seventeenth-century French philosopher, mathematician and physicist, Blaise Pascal says we are better off believing in God because if there is no God it doesn't matter whether we believe or not, but if there *is* a God our unbelief could land us in Hell.*

Third, there is the problem of being alone. Believing in God is the first step to having a relationship with God, and when you have a relationship with Him, you are never alone. If you don't believe in God you may feel quite alone in this world. Especially if you outlive your friends and family. My father, who at the age of 81 is a devout atheist, feels no need to have God in his life, but he does complain that it is sad that so many of his friends have died. I asked him if believing in God and the possibility of an afterlife would make him feel better. He said he wasn't sure.

Fourth, believing in God helps one believe that somehow, everything is going to work out in the end as there is Someone who is looking out for you. A loving parent who knows all about your struggles, a parent who will be with you while you are going through them, and who will

---

* Woody Allen points out how shocked some of us will be if we wind up in heaven or hell and find out it's what the Bible taught, only to exclaim "They told me in college that all of this was bullshit!"

ultimately bring you out of them. Belief in God not only provides meaning in life, it gives you Someone to lean on in difficult times.

Finally, believing in God is a path to humility, as it recognizes that there is something greater than ourselves.

❧

Exercise: Write down the reasons to believe in God and the reasons not to. Then re-examine your own belief system and see what makes the most sense for you.

The Eight Paths Of Blessing God

We now come to the final section of *It's* Not *all About You!*: Blessing God. What can you give to an Omnipotent, Omnipresent, Omniscient Being? To the One who Created Everything in the Universe, including you? If you've faithfully practiced the paths in the previous section on Blessing Others, you are already doing good for those other humans who were created in God's image and are already pleasing God by doing so.

As we've mentioned several times before, Jesus said that all of the laws boil down to loving God and other human beings. In the previous section we've already seen how the path of serving others blesses them, now we're going to focus on 8 ways to bless God.

The Path Of Seeking God's Approval, Not Man's

"Seek ye first the kingdom of God and His righteousness
and all these things shall be added unto you"

– Matthew 6:33

As we've seen, today society has us asking ourselves two basic questions: "What can I get out of life—and am I getting enough?" and "What do other people think of me?" As we just discussed, changing the first question to "What can I *give* to life—and am I *giving* enough?" puts us back on the right track, turning our selfishness into selflessness. Likewise, changing the second question to "What does GOD think of me?"* helps us live life with integrity and keeps us from worrying about our "image" to men and women who may judge us unfairly.

When you stop seeking other people's approval, you are free from the self-consciousness that plagues our generation. Other people don't know you the way God does. They don't see your inner struggles. They don't know what motivates you. They don't know your potential. They don't know your destiny.

Only God knows these things. And if you believe—as I do—in a compassionate God, you won't have to worry about being judged too harshly either.

But, you may ask, "How do we really know what God thinks of us?" While it might seem most un-humble to speak for God, as a pastor I actually *do* speak for God when I preach, and I would say categorically that God loves us. As for how we please Him, the answer is, again, love. After all, virtually every religion encourages us to do two things: Love

---

* Atheist readers can substitute "What do **I** think of me?" for "What does GOD think of me?" This, though not perfect, is a quantum leap above "What do others think of me?" For while we don't know ourselves as well as God does, we certainly know ourselves and our motivations better than others do.

others and love God. Jesus said all of the commandments in the Old Testament boiled down to "Love God" and "Love your neighbor as yourself." Other religions say much the same. LOVE is key. And that love is shown by being selfless. God designed us to give, and it's been shown that giving gives us the same chemical high we get from drugs and alcohol.

ᘓᘐ

Exercise: Go through your day noticing the temptation to worry about what others think of you. Then consciously think about how you can focus on what *God* thinks of you instead.

The Path Of Seeing Every Interaction As A Test From God, Every Task As An Assignment From God

Ultimately it is possible to see every situation as something conceived by God to teach you something and help you grow. In this sense life *is* actually "all about you"—all about you and God, that is. For while we've seen that thinking "it's all about you" is a grave mistake, as we develop a relationship with God and see Him at work in our lives, we can see His loving hand in every circumstance.

Sometimes this doesn't happen right away. As I was working on this book I wound up accidentally erasing four months' of work. At the time I was upset, but I utilized a number of the paths to humility found in this book and several that are to appear in the next book on accepting what we don't like about life. Then, after I rewrote the section that I'd lost, I realized the rewrite was much better than what I had before. God had just been acting as a good editor!

Mother Teresa adapted a version of a poem originally written by Kent M Keith called "Do It Anyway." The gist of the poem is that people may treat you badly even if you do good, but you should do good anyway because ultimately, everything is between you and God. So while the title of this book is *It's* Not *all About You!* in essence it IS all about you and God as every situation, every encounter is brought about by God to teach us something.

Do It Anyway

People are often unreasonable, irrational, and self-centered.
Forgive them anyway.
If you are kind, people may accuse you of selfish, ulterior motives.
Be kind anyway.

If you are successful, you will win
some unfaithful friends and some genuine enemies.
Succeed anyway.
If you are honest and sincere people may deceive you.
Be honest and sincere anyway.
What you spend years creating, others could destroy overnight.
Create anyway.
If you find serenity and happiness, some may be jealous.
Be happy anyway.
The good you do today, will often be forgotten.
Do good anyway.
Give the best you have, and it will never be enough.
Give your best anyway.
In the final analysis, it is between you and God.
It was never between you and them anyway.

Exercise: Try to look at the circumstances in your life as divinely ordered for your spiritual growth. Seek to understand what God is teaching you through the people and situations He puts in your path.

The Path Of Trusting God

As any parent knows, we want our children to trust us, and I believe God feels the same way. This is why the Bible says, "Without faith it is impossible to please Him." The more we trust in God and put Him in the center of our universe, the less worried and depressed we will be.

How would you feel if you were cradling your baby in your arms and she was afraid because she didn't believe you could protect her? I believe God's heart breaks whenever we don't trust Him to take care of us.

Our rational mind will always challenge us not to trust God. In Psalm 91 the Bible says "A thousand shall fall at thy side and ten thousand at thy right hand, but it shall not come nigh thee." Rationally, our survival instinct suggests that anything that can happen to someone else can happen to us as well. This is one reason not to watch the evening news, which often highlights the worst things that have happened to anyone over the past 24 hours.

There are ways to help us trust God more. These include being around fellow believers and listening to their testimonies of what God has done for them. It also helps to meditate on all that God has done for us. In particular how He has answered our prayers.

While they might seem small, two examples stand out. One was when I was in Cape Cod and foolishly dove into the ocean with my glasses on! (Brilliant, right?) When they vanished into the sea and couldn't be found, I suggested that my wife and son pray with me. Less than five minutes later my wife lifted her foot above the waves, the pair of glasses between her toes.

Another time we were in Jamaica and had lost the keys to the house and could not leave without them. Everyone was going crazy and blaming each other, so I just went and lay down in my bed and tried to stay positive. Then it occurred to me that I could pray. So I started praying and my wife walked in and said "Come on Dan, let's pray together." And, you guessed it, less than two minutes later the keys were found!

A much more impressive testimony came from the book I mentioned in The Path of Recognizing You Are Not Alone where I focused on "Godwinks." Here a pastor who was traveling across the country stopped at a gas station to fill his tank. As he was doing so, he heard a pay phone ringing. Thinking that it might be a call for the gas station attendant, he answered the phone, only to hear a woman's voice asking to speak to the pastor himself! As it turned out, the woman had seen the pastor on a TV show and was thinking about committing suicide and wanted desperately to speak to him. When the pastor asked how in the world she'd gotten that number, she said "It just came to me"—no doubt as a response to her desperate prayer.

Another way to learn to trust God is to read His Word and meditate on His promises. One which always lifts my spirit and helps me to trust Him is Romans 8:28 "All things work together for good to them that love God, to them that are the called according to His purpose." Not just the good things, but ALL things. When I remind myself that I serve a God who is all powerful, all knowing and exists everywhere, and I tie that to the promise of Romans 8:28, I get filled with faith. Yet, remarkably, I can go long periods of time forgetting this scripture completely.

A final way to trust God is to have intimate experiences of Him—something we'll discuss in The Path of Becoming One With God.

Trusting God is not always easy. Our rational minds and the world we live in don't encourage this trust, and Satan is quite happy to keep us from trusting our heavenly Father as well.

છ

Exercise: Write down all of the reasons God has given you to trust Him. Then look at this list whenever you're tempted to doubt Him.

The Path Of Obeying God

If one of the ways to trust God is to read His Word, it is also an excellent way to learn how to obey Him. For Jews, Christians and Muslims, the Bible and the Koran give us the rules to live by. Likewise Buddhists and Hindus have their holy scriptures as well.

Obedience has a very negative connotation in modern society, even more negative than the word "humility." I myself have a long history of rebellion against authority—a rebellion that showed itself in an article I wrote in my college yearbook where I mischaracterized Christianity as merely a religion of the Word that told us how to live (and, as such, was something I wanted no part of).

In the Bible there are 613 commandments in the Old Testament. The most well-known of these are the 10 commandments which Moses brought down from Mount Sinai. Yet Jesus says in the New Testament that you only need to follow two commandments and all the rest will follow. They are to love God with all of your heart, soul and mind, and to love your neighbor (that is, everybody) as yourself.

Of course loving God also means respecting Him and His commandments—at least those of His commandments that line up with the two mentioned by Christ (I don't think, for instance, that the commandment to stone rebellious teenagers found in the Old Testament lives up that standard —

although most of us who've raised a rebellious teenager have been tempted to indulge in the fantasy).

Christ's two laws also show the importance of what motivates our actions. For instance when theologian Dietrich Bonhoeffer tried to assassinate Adolph Hitler, it was to prevent loss of life, not take it. Likewise, we can perform the same exact action either out of a selfish motive or altruistic one, and our motivation makes all of the difference.

For example if you hit someone in the back because you want to harm them, it is entirely different than doing so because you think they're choking and you're trying to save their lives. So in the end, obedience simply comes down to taking action based on loving God and loving our fellow human beings.

This prescription, I believe, is something Judaism and Islam would agree with. For while Judaism is broken into reform, conservative and orthodox, with the orthodox adhering more closely to the letter of the law, motivation is still key. Islam means submission to God, and obedience to the teachings of Mohammed and Sharia Law are keys for Muslims as well. Neither would Buddhists or Hindus have a major problem with this, as both recognize the importance of acting out of right motives as a means of creating good karma.

Exercise: Do your best to be obedient to God today, acting out of the pure motive of trying to bless God and others.

The Path Of Becoming One With God
(Having A Spiritual Experience)

There is something beyond trusting God and obeying God. It is called "mysticism" and it means becoming One with God. While this may seem like something impossible to attain, I can assure you from personal experience that it is both possible and part of every major religion. While everyone can have this experience, it is, like life itself, a gift from God.

In every religion there is a group of people who want to have a closer relationship with The Almighty. Mystical Jews study the Kabbala. Mystical Christians catch the Holy Spirit. Mystical Muslims practice what's known as Sufism. Buddhists experience their "Buddha Nature" and Hindus enter Nirvana. Many mystics believe that they are able to have a direct experience of God because they believe that God Himself is the center of their Being.

I wrote a long article in my college yearbook called "Academica Philosophica Mystica" where I shared some of the basics of Eastern thought with my college buddies in an attempt to fill a gross gap in our ivy league education. An education that included several required courses on Western Civilization but only offered courses on Eastern Civilization as electives in the religion department—courses which very few of my fellow Columbians ever took. I used that article to share a number of the works on Eastern thought and mysticism which had shaped my walk with God.

Recently I had the opportunity to revisit that work, as someone in my 35th reunion dinner pulled out a yearbook. Two things I noticed. One, that my writing hadn't improved much in 35 years despite earning a Master's in Journalism; and two, that I had grossly mischaracterized Christianity as a religion that did not include mainstream mysticism.

After all, Christians are always talking about experiencing or ("catching") the Holy Spirit, which, in essence, is God Himself.

෴

Exercise: Pick up a book on mysticism—or better yet, a book such as *The Bagavad Gita, The Platform Sutra of the Sixth Patriarch* or the poems of Jalal al-Din Rumi. See if they help you have a Transformative Experience.

The Path Of Loving God

If you've ever had a personal experience of God's Love like those described in the previous path, you know that God loves you more than any human ever could. But even if you just know Him through the scriptures or the Beauty of His Creation, when you stop and realize how much God loves you, the only sane option is to love Him back. When you understand that you and I, as small and imperfect as we are, are important to the Almighty Creator of this vast universe, you realize what a privilege it is to be able to worship Him. That God loves us despite knowing all of our flaws is a deeply humbling thought, and while I can't speak for you, it makes me want to love Him even more.

The Bible insists that love itself is the highest virtue of all—and that nothing you do is valuable if you don't do it out of love.

As 1 Corinthians Chapter 13 states:

> "Though I speak with the tongues of men and of angels, but have not love, I have become sounding brass or a clanging cymbal. And though I have the gift of prophecy, and understand all mysteries and all knowledge, and though I have all faith, so that I could remove mountains, but have not love, I am nothing. And though I bestow all my goods to feed the poor, and though I give my body to be burned, but have not love, it profits me nothing.
>
> Love suffers long and is kind; love does not envy; love does not parade itself, is not puffed up; does not behave rudely, does not seek its own, is not provoked, thinks no evil; does not rejoice in iniquity, but rejoices

in the truth; bears all things, believes all things, hopes all things, endures all things.

Love never fails. But whether there are prophecies, they will fail; whether there are tongues, they will cease; whether there is knowledge, it will vanish away. For we know in part and we prophesy in part. But when that which is perfect has come, then that which is in part will be done away.

When I was a child, I spoke as a child, I understood as a child, I thought as a child; but when I became a man, I put away childish things. For now we see in a mirror, dimly, but then face to face. Now I know in part, but then I shall know just as I also am known.

And now abide faith, hope, love, these three; but the greatest of these is love."

∞

Exercise: Focus on the thought that Almighty God, Creator of the Universe, loves you dearly despite all of your flaws. Now love Him back for loving you.

The Path Of Crucifying Self: A.K.A. "Sanctification"

When I first started having mystical experiences, I thought I was the only one who'd ever had them and that this enlightenment was the highest state a human could achieve. And while I was wrong about being the only one who'd ever tasted Spiritual Reality, I was only partially right about this being the highest goal in life. For while it is indeed the highest *state*, there is something more. Something hinted at in the previous paths of trusting and obeying God.

For there is enlightenment (that is, having a direct experience of God) and then there is Enlightenment with a capital "E": that is, living the life in accordance to what we experience in those precious mountaintop moments. This is the way of the Tao and the practice of Zen, both of which focus on living each moment as a spiritually awakened individual. In fact, it is something that every Jew, Christian, Muslim, Hindu and Buddhist aspires to: To live an upright life that is pleasing to God. In Christianity Jesus Christ is the example, as He was always in the moment, never in a hurry, and always doing His Father's will. For while we are not called to sacrifice our lives to death on a cross, we are to sacrifice our lives by *living* a life that is dedicated to serving God and others.

That is, to sacrifice our selfish desires and live for God and our fellow human beings. This ongoing work of sanctification does not stop until we die.

For those who are proud to be Christians and are right now doing their version of Saturday Night Live's Church Lady Superior Dance, I would remind you of what Maya Angelou said to people who came up to her and introduced themselves as Christians. "So soon?" she would say, alluding to the fact that living up to the ideals of Christ's teachings is a lifelong process.

Are you willing to give up your right to yourself? Ironically, our willingness to give up what we think will make us happy makes us happy in the end. Giving up our right to ourselves, to whatever extent we are able to do it, is the key to a humility that gives us lasting peace. This is no easy task, as the addiction to self may well be the strongest addiction of all. But while there's no patch to get rid of the cravings, we can, through humility, overcome our self-addiction.

$$\infty$$

Exercise: Look for ways today to give up your right to yourself in whatever part of your life where you feel God is asking you to make a sacrifice. Seek His will and turn your life over to it.

The Path Of Accepting Christ As Lord And Savior

If crucifying self is the next-to-the-last path to humility, turning your life over to the One who was crucified for you is the final path to humility I want you to consider.

I realize that accepting Jesus Christ as Lord and Savior is not a path every reader will take, and that some will be offended that I even mention it as an option. While I find it odd that people in a nation founded by Christians are more offended by the word "Christ" than they are of the word "Buddha," I realize this has something to do with some insensitive Christians who have tried to force their majority views on others.

While movements like the Crusades, where Christians killed non-Christians allegedly to save their souls from going to Hell, and the Spanish Inquisition, where Jews and other nonbelievers were tortured until they accepted Christ or died, today most Christians who try to share their faith are acting out of love for nonbelievers and obeying the words of Christ at the end of the Gospel of Matthew to teach and baptize "all nations."

After all, sharing our faith is dicey business. In some countries, Christians who share their faith risk jail, torture or even death. American Christians like myself run the risk of rejection, for, as some have noted, the quickest way to end a conversation in America is to mention Jesus. That's why I saved this path for last.

Still, at the risk that you will burn this book and post bad evaluations of it on Amazon, I wouldn't be doing my duty as a Christian minister if I didn't at least *offer* the path of Eternal Salvation in a book filled with paths to humility. For one of the greatest paths to humility is to accept Jesus as Lord and Savior, as humbling oneself before another man—albeit one who was God as well as man—takes great humility. But the benefits are "out of this world."*

---

* These are the exact words used by the principle/owner of a Christian elementary school where I was applying to teach to describe the benefits package which did not

While I have no heaven or hell to put you in, the Bible says that the way to assure ourselves of Eternal Life in heaven after we die is to accept Christ as our Lord and Savior. So that, when we go before the judgment seat of God and the devil tries to claim us for himself, citing the sins we've committed and how we belong with him in Hell, Jesus, as our advocate, will, like a lawyer in the courtroom, step in and say that we belong with Him in heaven because He paid the price for our sins when He died on the Cross.

The great Christian writer C.S. Lewis states that, "Only people who know they need forgiveness have any use for Christianity." Those of you who have been reading this book carefully should now realize that part of humility is recognizing that none of us are perfect and that we all need forgiveness.

Accepting Christ is an act of humility. I used to think there was no man I would ever bow down to. While Christ is God incarnate, to surrender oneself to Him requires a certain amount of humility. For not only are you pledging your allegiance to a Lord, you are admitting that you can't handle all of your problems on your own. That you need and accept Christ as your Lord and Savior for paying the price for your sins on a cross on Calvary 2,000 plus years ago.

Beyond the obvious benefits of knowing you are heaven-bound, salvation is about having a relationship with a Spiritual Being. A relationship which can be tangible, as those who've felt His Spirit can attest.

❧

Exercise: If you would like to start a relationship with Christ (to be, as they say "saved") just say these words: "I believe that Jesus Christ is the Son of God and that He died for my sins. I accept Him as my Lord and Savior."

---

include health insurance. I turned the job down and went to another Christian school whose benefits were in this world as well out of it.

CONCLUSION

Thank you for the honor of reading this book. I encourage you to re-read the paths as often as you like so that you may recall them when needed.

Blessings.

APPENDIX A

The Humility Paths
(Or "Mental Happiness Tools")
And The Exercises That Go With Them

Path to Humility #1: The Path of Recognizing It's Not All About You

Exercise #1: Reflect on what ways you are making life all about you. How could you remind yourself that, while you have an important role to play in other people's lives, you are not the center of their universe?

Path to Humility #2: Recognizing Others Are "Other Me's"

Exercise #2: Think about how other people—especially any you consider your "enemies"—are really other "you's" in different bodies. Reflect on the fact that if you were in their shoes, you would likely be making the same bad choices they are making.

Path to Humility #3: The Path of Lowering Our Expectations of What Others Can Do For Us

Exercise #3: The next time you attend a social event with people that make you uneasy, lower your expectations.

Path to Humility #4: The Path of Having Compassion For Others

Exercise #4: Practice an act of compassion today, doing something for someone else—one that doesn't benefit you in any way. This could mean giving to charity, or giving a dollar to someone who is selling a newspaper or asking for spare change.

Path to Humility #5: The Path of Driving a Humble Automobile

Exercise #5: Buy a cheap car.

Path to Humility #6: The Path of Dressing Humbly

Exercise #6: Try dressing down for a day. Notice how this affects your humility.

Path to Humility #7: The Path of Treating People Like People and Not By Their Titles

Exercise #7: Remind yourself that we are all human beings no matter what our position in society. Make a conscious effort to treat each individual you meet today with the respect they deserve regardless of their title or lack thereof.

Path to Humility #8: Recognizing The Difference Between Judging and Evaluating

Exercise #8: Think about those people who you have some complaint about. Then remind yourself that they are "other me's" and avoid the temptation to judge them.

Path to Humility #9: The First Reason to Stop Judging: The Path of Recognizing We Don't Know Enough About Them

Exercise #9: As you are tempted to judge others throughout the course of your day, remind yourself that you don't know enough about that person to judge him or her.

Path to Humility #10: The Second Reason to Stop Judging: The Path of Recognizing We Do The Same Things As Those We Judge

Exercise #10: When someone's behavior irritates you today, ask yourself how you may be guilty of the same thing. Then forgive them and let the ill-effects of their behavior evaporate like water off a duck's back.

Path to Humility #11: The Third Reason to Stop Judging: The Path of Recognizing Others May Be Living Up To Their Potential More Than We Are

Exercise: Look at the people who you judge as being spiritually immature. Now remember that those same people 1) may be more mature than you think, and 2) may be living up to their potential more than you—even if you are right about them being less mature than you are.

Path to Humility #12: The Fourth Reason to Stop Judging: The Path of Recognizing That We Shouldn't Judge Others Because We Don't Want To Be Judged

Exercise #12: Whenever you are tempted to judge someone, remind yourself that you don't want to be judged harshly and that the less you judge others, the less you will be judged.

Path to Humility #13: The Path of Forgiving Others

Exercise #13: Think of all the people in your life who you consider "enemies." Then forgive them and pray for them as if they were your closest friends, remembering the example of Nelson Mandela, the concentration camp victim, and Jesus on the cross. (If you don't believe in prayer, wish them well.)

Path to Humility #14: The Path of Going Beyond Forgiveness and Responding to Mistreatment with Humble Love

Exercise #14: The next time someone does something you don't like, respond with kindness. If it doesn't change the other person, at least you can go on with your life feeling good about yourself.

Path to Humility #15: The Path of Not Feeling Superior Because of Our Political or Religious Beliefs

Exercise #15: Talk to someone of another religious faith about their beliefs, read one of their holy books or visit one of their holy places.

Path to Humility #16: The Path of "I Used To Be Disgusted But Now I Try To Be Amused"

Exercise #16: When someone—or something—tempts you to get angry today, remind yourself of the wisdom of Elvis Costello's "I used to be disgusted, and now I try to be amused." If that doesn't work, look at your negative reaction with compassion and try to be amused at the fact that you weren't able to be amused in the first place. If that doesn't work, take a double shot of Jack Daniels (just kidding church folk! ;-).

You may also choose to do what one of my clients did and write down all of the stupid stuff others say and do to you—then go back and read it and see how ridiculous it was. My client said this helped him deal with the hassles of living in a homeless shelter.

Path to Humility #17: The Path Of Not Taking Ourselves Too Seriously

Exercise #17: The next time you're disgusted with yourself for something you've done, remind yourself of your humanity and find something amusing in your own bad behavior—or your insistence on being "perfect."

Path to Humility #18: The Path of Recognizing You're Only Human

Exercise #18: Take a fearless moral inventory of yourself, writing down all of your faults and taking a good hard look at yourself. If you are a Christian, consider your sins and recognize that they were the reason Jesus had to die on the Cross.

Path to Humility #19: The Path of Self-Deprecating Humor

Exercise #19: Look back on something you've done in your life that was embarrassing and try to find the humor in it. Better yet, next time the opportunity arises, make fun of yourself in public and notice the reaction you get.

Path to Humility #20: The Path of Comparing Ourselves To Those Who Gave More

Exercise #20: Compare yourself to the Spiritual giants and ask yourself in what small way you could be more like them today.

Path to Humility #21: The Path of Recognizing How Little We Know Ourselves

Exercise #21: Think about what you know—and what you don't know—about yourself. Feel the humility that comes from letting go of a false sense of solidity.

Path to Humility #22: The Path Of Recognizing Our Rightful Place In The Universe—Part I: Little "i"s In A Great Big Universe

Exercise #22: Remind yourself how small you are compared to the rest of the universe.

Path to Humility #23: The Path of Recognizing Our Rightful Place in the Universe Part II: The Path of Recognizing You Are Not Alone

Exercise #23: As you go through your day remind yourself that you are but one of billions of people living on a small planet in the middle of outer space. Use this to help you put your problems (I mean "challenges") in perspective.

Path to Humility #24: The Path of Recognizing How Little We Know

Exercise #24a: Think back to your childhood and think of the things you used to hold as gospel truth but you now know are patently false. If you didn't have ludicrous discussions about tennis balls, remember what you thought about Santa Claus and the Tooth Fairy. Or where you thought babies came from. Then remember that much of what you think is true right now will turn out to be false. Let go of false solidity and humble yourself accordingly.

Exercise #24b: As you go through the day, think about those things we take for granted—and recognize that much of it is going to turn out to be rubbish.

Path to Humility #25: The Path of Developing A Healthy Relationship With Death

Exercise #25: Stop and think about all the problems that could arise if there were no death. Then be grateful for its existence.

Path to Humility #26: The Path of Not Wasting What Could Be Your Last Thought On Planet Earth on Something Negative

Exercise #26: View the negative thoughts that go through your mind through the prism of your mortality, challenging yourself not to waste your time on them.

Path to Humility #27: The Path of Living Like This Could Be Your Last Day On Planet Earth

Exercise #27: Live today as if it could be your last day on earth, savoring every interaction as the special gift it is.

Path to Humility #28: The Path of Recognizing We Are Not In Control

Exercise #28: Think about how little control we truly have over how long we will be on this earth. Then, instead of giving into fear, embrace it, reminding yourself that trying to control what cannot be controlled is counterproductive.

Path to Humility #29: The Path of Having Faith That Everything Will Be Alright

Exercise #29: Remind yourself that you've been taken care of by God/ the Universe for all of your life thus far. Now trust these cosmic forces to keep you in the future as well. Have faith that death is not necessarily the end of your Existence.

Path to Humility #30: The Path of Recognizing What We Can and Cannot Control: The First Paradox of Control

Exercise #30: Remember that a trained mind can withstand severe circumstances while an untrained mind is bothered by the slightest disturbance. Vow to train your mind and start meditating, developing a prayer ritual or reading books like the ones recommended in this book that help you train your mind (this could include reading and re-reading the paths in this book so they become second nature).

Path to Humility #31: The Path of Controlling What CAN be controlled (The Benefits of a Disciplined Mind)

Exercise #31: Consider The Serenity Prayer of A.A. substituting "humility" for "serenity."

Lord, give me the <u>humility</u> to accept the things I cannot change

The courage to change the things I can

And the wisdom to know the difference

Path to Humility #32: The Path of Being Less Controlled by Others and External Events By Relinquishing Our Desire to Control Them

Exercise #32: Stop trying to control what cannot be controlled. This includes not being disturbed by past events and not projecting negative experiences in the future. Remind yourself that the less you try to control what you cannot, the less control events and other people have over you.

Path to Humility #33: The Path of Not Worrying About The Wellbeing of Others: A Personal Confession

Exercise #33: Remember that you are not responsible for other people's welfare and give up worrying about situations involving loved ones that you cannot help them with. This does not mean abandoning your responsibilities, it just means recognizing your limitations.

Path to Humility #34: The Path of Recognizing Our Inability to Control Our Lives And Turning Them Over To a Higher Power

Exercise #34: Recognize your limitations as a finite mortal and turn your life over to your Higher Power.

Path to Humility #35: The Path of Taking Responsibility for the Limited Control We Have Over Our Lives

Exercise #35: Recognize that you have limited control over your life and use your will to benefit yourself and others to whatever extent possible.

Path to Humility #36: The Path of Appreciating What You Have More Rather Than Looking For More To Appreciate

Exercise #36: Go through your day focusing on appreciating what you have more.

Path to Humility #37: The Path of Thinking About How Much Good Karma We Can Create In The Day (In The Hopes of a Blessing In This Life or The Afterlife)

Exercise #37: Think of ways to create good karma for yourself today, reminding yourself it will benefit you in the long run.

Path to Humility #38: The Path of Doing Good for Goodness Sake

Exercise #38: Do something good for someone else today without expecting anything in return.

Path to Humility #39: The Path of Not Being In a Hurry

Exercise #39: Let someone ahead of you in a grocery line. Relax and meditate or enjoy the music on your radio when stuck in a traffic jam. Pray for the driver who cuts you off in traffic.

Path to Humility #40: The Path of Listening

Exercise #40: Be mindful not to cut someone off when you're talking to them. Take time to really listen to someone else today.

Path to Humility #41: The Path of Letting Go of Pride

Exercise #41: Humble yourself and let go of your unhealthy pride.

Path to Humility #42: The Path of Recognizing We're Not Really THAT Spiritually Advanced

In *Essential Teachings*, the Dalai Lama warns against following the "eight principles." These are: love of praise; rejection of blame; desiring gain; fearing loss; liking comfort and luxury; fearing discomfort and poverty; taking in all that is pleasant; rejecting all that is painful.

Exercise #42: Hold your life up to the above standard and humble yourself accordingly.

Path to Humility #43: The Path of Not Taking Credit

Exercise #43: Do something good today for which you will get no credit whatsoever.

Path to Humility #44: The Path of Recognizing You Are The Product of a Champion Sperm and a Precious Egg

Exercise #44: If you find yourself feeling down at any point today, remind yourself that you are a miracle. A one in a zillion product of a long line of champion sperm and special eggs. Then remind yourself that everyone you meet today is just such a champion as well—and treat them that way.

Path to Humility #45: The Path of Recognizing That You Are The Pinnacle of Evolution

Exercise #45: Think about how long it took God to create the universe and put humans on this earth. Reflect on the fact that you are the result of that evolution.

Path to Humility #46: The Path of Recognizing That You Are The Center of God's Creation

Exercise #46: Remind yourself how much God loves you. Reflect on the fact that you are His child and that He is your Father.

Path to Humility #47: The Path of Recognizing Your Worth to Others

Exercise #47: Write down some of the things you've done for others or that others have told you you've done for them. Look at this list every time your self-esteem needs a boost.

Path to Humility #48: The Path of Looking at Ourselves as Glasses That are Half Full

Exercise #48: Just as the previous challenge was to write down what you've done for others, this time I'd like you to make a list of your good qualities and accomplishments. If you can't think of any (and, yes, I've actually had clients who said they can't think of a single positive about themselves), ask a friend or a loved one to help you out. Then read it back to yourself when you need a boost—or read the poem by Max Ehrmann called Desiderata (see attached).

Path to Humility #49: The Path of Recognizing Our Wants are Not Our Needs

Exercise #49: Pay attention to your anxiety. Then ask yourself if the anxiety is coming from treating something you want as if it were something you need. Remind yourself that your wants are not your needs.

Path to Humility #50: The Path of Expecting Less and Getting More

Exercise #50: Lower your unrealistic expectations about life and be humbly grateful for all of the blessings you receive.

Path to Humility #51: The Path of Not Expecting Heaven On Earth

Exercise #51: If you've been expecting heaven on earth, right-size your expectations about life on planet earth. Instead of being bitter that life is not perfect, be grateful for all of the positive experiences you have.

Path to Humility #52: The Path of Letting Go of the Melodrama of the Mind

Exercise #52: Recognize that you are not the voice in your head or your feelings; that you are the one who hears these thoughts and feels these emotions. If you have the time, read *The Untethered Soul*.

Path to Humility #53: The Path of Giving Up The Part of You That Needs Protecting

Exercise #53: Use your humility to keep from fighting life today. Instead of being two people—the self who needs protection and the one who is protecting your self-image—allow yourself just to experience life with gratitude, not worrying about having to defend yourself at all. Allow yourself the freedom just to accept life as it comes.

Path to Humility #54: The Path of Thinking About How Events Are Good For Others Instead of How They Affect You

Exercise #54: Think about those areas of your life where you've let "self" creep in. Now go through your day staying other- and God-focused, applying the humility that allows you not to think of yourself at all.

Path to Humility #55: The Path of Renouncing The Little Mafioso In Your Head

Exercise #55: The next time the little Mafioso in your head pops up, remind yourself of the following three quotes which I've mentioned earlier in this audiobook but are worth repeating:

Of some thoughts one stands perplexed—especially at the sight of men's sin—and wonders whether one should use force or humble love. Always decide to use humble love. If you resolve on that, once and for all, you may subdue the whole world. Loving humility is marvelously strong, and strongest of all things, and there is nothing else like it."

—Fyodor Dostoyevsky

Humility is a willingness to be underestimated or slighted and feel no resentment.

—Peter Wagner

O Lord, Remember not only the men and women of good will but all those of ill will. But do not remember all the suffering they have inflicted upon us; remember the fruits we have bought thanks to this suffering—our comradeship, our loyalty, our humility, our courage, our generosity, the greatness of heart which has grown out of all this; and when they come to judgment, let all the fruits we have borne be their forgiveness.

—Found in Concentration Camp for women prisoners in Nazi Germany

Path to Humility #56: The Path of Recognizing Others Are More Worried About What You Think of Them Than They Are Busy Judging You

Exercise #56: The next time you find yourself uncomfortable at a social event, remind yourself that everyone else is more focused on what folks are thinking about them than they are focused on you.

Path to Humility #57: The Path of Not Worrying About Yourself

Exercise #57: Remember the following quotes whenever you are feeling tempted to worry:

"A man goes to knowledge as a man goes to war: Wide awake, with fear, with respect and with absolute assurance."

—*Carlos Casteneda*, The Teachings of Don Juan

"If you're bothered by the future, you're making up a future that doesn't exist that bothers you."

—*Michael Singer*

"Everything will be okay as soon as you are okay with everything—and that's the only time everything will be okay."

—*Michael Singer*

"All things work together for good to them that love God, to those who are the called according to His purpose."

—Romans 8:28

"For God has not given us the spirit of fear, but of power, and of love, and of a sound mind."

—2 Timothy 1:7

Path to Humility #58: The Path of Thinking of Others' Needs as Well as Our Own

Exercise #58: Focus on what others around you want and/or need from you today, thinking of how much good you can do for others in the next 24 hours.

Path to Humility #59: The Path of Being Nice to Others

Exercise #59: Go out of your way to do something nice for someone else, and make a point of complimenting someone at work or at home.

Path to Humility #60: The Path of Serving Others

Exercise #60: "Wash someone's feet" today by serving them in whatever way you can find.

Path to Humility #61: The Path of Seeking To Give More Than You Get

Exercise #61: Look at your schedule for the next week and see where you can give more than you get. Where you can put others' needs above yours—or where you can meet someone else's needs in a way that blesses you as well.

Path to Humility #62: The Path of Believing in God

Exercise #62: Write down the reasons to believe in God and the reasons not to. Then re-examine your own belief system and see what makes the most sense for you.

Path to Humility #63: The Path of Seeking God's Approval, Not Man's

Exercise #63: Go through your day noticing the temptation to worry about what others think of you. Then consciously think about how you can focus on what *God* thinks of you instead.

Path to Humility #64: The Path of Seeing Every Interaction as a Test From God, Every Task as an Assignment From God

Exercise #64: Try to look at the circumstances in your life as divinely ordered for your spiritual growth. Seek to understand what God is teaching you through the people and situations He puts in your path.

Path to Humility #65: The Path of Trusting God

Exercise #65: Write down all of the reasons God has given you to trust Him. Then look at this list whenever you're tempted to doubt Him.

Path to Humility #66: The Path of Obeying God

Exercise #66: Do your best to be obedient to God today, acting out of the pure motive of trying to bless God and others.

Path to Humility #67: The Path of Becoming One with God (Having a Spiritual Experience)

Exercise #67: Pick up a book on mysticism—or better yet, a book such as *The Bagavad Gita, The Platform Sutra of the Sixth Patriarch* or the poems of Jalal al-Din Rumi. See if they help you have a Transformative Experience.

Path to Humility #68: The Path of Loving God

Exercise #68: Focus on the thought that Almighty God, Creator of the Universe, loves you dearly despite all of your flaws. Now love Him back for loving you.

Path to Humility #69: The Path of Crucifying Self: A.K.A. "Sanctification"

Exercise #69: Look for ways today to give up your right to yourself in whatever part of your life where you feel God is asking you to make a sacrifice. Seek His will and turn your life over to it.

Path to Humility #70: The Path of Accepting Christ As Lord and Savior

Exercise #70: If you would like to start a relationship with Christ (to be, as they say "saved") just say these words: "I believe that Jesus Christ is the Son of God and that He died for my sins. I accept Him as my Lord and Savior."

APPENDIX B

Recommended Spiritual Reading

The Untethered Soul by Michael Singer

Essential Teachings by the Dalai Lama

Twelve Steps and Twelve Traditions by Bill Wilson

The Seven Spiritual Laws of Success by Deepak Chopra

The Platform Sutra of the Sixth Patriarch by Hui Neng

Present Moment, Wonderful Moment by Thich Nhat Hanh

The Bagavad Gita

The Poems of Jalal Ad-Din Rumi

The Holy Bible (recommending "The Open Bible" study version)

The Message (Bible remix) by Eugene Paterson

Mere Christianity by C.S. Lewis

The Teachings of Don Juan: A Yaqui Way of Knowledge by Carlos Casteneda

Autobiography of a Yogi – Yogananda

The Holy Quran – The Prophet Muhammed

The Tao Te Ching – Lao-tzu

My Utmost For His Highest – Oswald Chambers

The Practice of Presence – Patty de Llosa

APPENDIX C

TWO POEMS FOR SPIRITUAL GROWTH

DESIDERATA

Go placidly amid the noise and haste,
and remember what peace there may be in silence.
As far as possible without surrender
be on good terms with all persons.
Speak your truth quietly and clearly;
and listen to others,
even the dull and the ignorant;
they too have their story.
Avoid loud and aggressive persons,
they are vexations to the spirit.
If you compare yourself with others,
you may become vain and bitter;
for always there will be greater and lesser persons than yourself.
Enjoy your achievements as well as your plans.
Keep interested in your own career, however humble;
it is a real possession in the changing fortunes of time.
Exercise caution in your business affairs;
for the world is full of trickery.
But let this not blind you to what virtue there is;
many persons strive for high ideals;
and everywhere life is full of heroism.
Be yourself.
Especially, do not feign affection.
Neither be cynical about love;
for in the face of all aridity and disenchantment
it is as perennial as the grass.

Take kindly the counsel of the years,
gracefully surrendering the things of youth.
Nurture strength of spirit to shield you in sudden misfortune.
But do not distress yourself with dark imaginings.
Many fears are born of fatigue and loneliness.
Beyond a wholesome discipline,
be gentle with yourself.
You are a child of the universe,
no less than the trees and the stars;
you have a right to be here.
And whether or not it is clear to you,
no doubt the universe is unfolding as it should.
Therefore be at peace with God,
whatever you conceive Him to be,
and whatever your labors and aspirations,
in the noisy confusion of life keep peace with your soul.
With all its sham, drudgery, and broken dreams,
it is still a beautiful world.
Be cheerful.
Strive to be happy.

Max Ehrmann, Desiderata

Do It Anyway

People are often unreasonable, irrational, and self-centered.
Forgive them anyway.
If you are kind, people may accuse you of selfish, ulterior motives.
Be kind anyway.
If you are successful, you will win
some unfaithful friends and some genuine enemies.
Succeed anyway.
If you are honest and sincere people may deceive you.
Be honest and sincere anyway.
What you spend years creating, others could destroy overnight.
Create anyway.
If you find serenity and happiness, some may be jealous.
Be happy anyway.
The good you do today, will often be forgotten.
Do good anyway.
Give the best you have, and it will never be enough.
Give your best anyway.
In the final analysis, it is between you and God.
It was never between you and them anyway.

(**This** poem, often attributed to Mother Teresa, was originally written by Kent M. Keith.)

APPENDIX D

Some Excellent Quotations About Humility

"Humility does not mean thinking less of yourself than of other people, nor does it mean having a low opinion of your own gifts. It means freedom from thinking about yourself at all."

—William Temple

"Humility is like underwear, essential, but indecent if it shows."

— Helen Nielsen

"No labor, however humble, is dishonoring"

— The Talmud

"The most powerful weapon to conquer evil is humility. For evil does not know at all how to employ it, nor does it know how to defend itself against it."

— St. Vincent de Paul

"Humility leads to strength and not to weakness. It is the highest form of self-respect to admit mistakes and to make amends for them."

— John McCloy

"When science discovers the center of the universe, a lot of people will be disappointed to find they are not it."

— Bernard Baily

"Once the game is over, the king and the pawn go back in the same box."

— Italian proverb

"O Lord, Remember not only the men and women of good will but all those of ill will. But do not remember all the suffering they have inflicted upon us; remember the fruits we have bought thanks to this suffering—our comradeship, our loyalty, our humility, our courage, our generosity, the greatness of heart which has grown out of all this; and when they come to judgment, let all the fruits we have borne be their forgiveness."

— FOUND IN THE RAVENSBRUCK CONCENTRATION CAMP

"Self-conceit shows a lack of sensibility and maturity. Those who are more reflective and spiritually mature have the sense to attribute whatever gifts they may have to the Creator, the Most High, and devote themselves to him with humble gratitude."

— M. FETHULLA GULEN

"Of some thoughts one stands perplexed—especially at the sight of men's sin—and wonders whether one should use force or humble love. Always decide to use humble love. If you resolve on that, once and for all, you may subdue the whole world. Loving humility is marvelously strong, and strongest of all things, and there is nothing else like it."

— FYODOR DOSTOYEVSKY

"There is no limit to what can be done if it doesn't matter who gets the credit."

— AUTHOR UNKNOWN

"Humility is a willingness to be underestimated or slighted and feel no resentment."

— Peter Wagner, *Humility*

ABOUT THE AUTHOR

Daniel Aaron Cohen

Daniel Aaron Cohen is child of God whose main mission in life is to spread God's Love throughout the world. He currently pastors Congregational Church of Burlington, Connecticut, and is a graduate of Columbia University, where he majored in Eastern Religion. He also holds Master's degrees in Journalism from Northwestern University, in Divinity from New York Theological Seminary, and in Social Work from Fordham University. In addition to pastoring, he is a psychotherapist in private practice, and previously worked as a journalist and as a teacher at the grade school, high school and college levels. He is married to his lovely wife Christine and has two sons, Jason and Samuel, as well as two granddaughters, Miracle and Serenity.

Daniel is currently working on a book of Lenten Humility Devotionals and, rather ironically for an author who dares to tackle humility, an autobiography, as well as two other books on the paths to humility that he discovered in the 10-plus years he has been looking for them. They are: 1) Paths that focus on ACCEPTING everything we don't like about life and 2) Paths that focus on being GRATEFUL for everything we do like about life.

Stay up to date on Daniel and his future books by visiting his website at DanielAaronCohen.com.